Raising Children to Thrive

Copyright © 2024 by Ronald Ruff

All rights reserved.

ISBN 978-1-960378-17-0 (hardcover)

ISBN 978-1-960378-18-7 (paperback)

ISBN 978-1-960378-19-4 (eBook)

1st Edition

Design by Anna Hall

For my parents, Samuel and Harriett,
my brother, Ned,
my wife, Zaneta,
our children, Mara, Miriam, and Rebecca
and our grandchildren, Zachary, Jordyn, Ari, and Alex

"From generation to generation"

Raising Children to Thrive:

Affect Hunger and Responsive, Sensitive Parenting

RONALD RUFF, PhD

ACKNOWLEDGEMENTS

I wrote this book for several reasons.

First and foremost, after retiring, I wanted to find a way to continue to help others. I felt that writing a book would satisfy that desire while also allowing the writer in me to emerge. I concluded that, after fifty years of listening to thousands of people, it was finally time for me to speak in my own voice.

Second, after thinking about my field and conducting extensive research, I realized that some dramatic new findings have occurred since I first started. It was then that I decided to provide those findings in a manner that might positively influence parenting and child development. As Toni Morrison said, "If there's a book that you want to read, but it hasn't been written yet, then you must write it."

And then it hit me: I was also writing this book for a deeper, very personal, previously unknown reason. I wrote this book for you, yes, but also for my children, Mara, Miriam, and Rebecca, and for my wife, Zaneta. To my wife and children, let me just say that this project represents my own way of telling you what I did with my many years of working as a psychologist. After all, having to maintain confidentiality throughout my career, I could not discuss my work. In high school, I had friends whose ironworker fathers would take them to Chicago to watch them top off a skyscraper with high steel. This book is my skyscraper. It is, in a real sense, how I constructed my own life. The many floors and five years of daily toil are finally worthy of being seen, and more importantly, occupied. In these pages, my dear family, you can see the results of my life's work, at least in part. I feel like a spy who has finally come in from the cold.

I am very proud to be your father and to have raised you alongside your mother. I enjoyed coaching your baseball teams, watching you ice skate, swim, play your flute, violins, sing in the choir, play with your friends, ski with you, take you to the library, hear you laugh, and just be with you. Now, I continue to feel joy watching you all as successful professional women in your chosen fields, functioning as self-fulfilled, kind, loving, compassionate people, raising your own children as amazing mothers and or being a wonderful aunt. I am so proud of you.

So I want to thank you and Mom. The untold joy I felt then, and even more now, of having you in my lives, gave me the strength and relief to continue to help others who were in pain and suffering.

Next, to my father, who taught me—by example and in words—to treat everyone with the same dignity and respect, that I can learn from anyone, and to always be myself, please know that you and your gentle strength, wisdom, and love live within me.

To my mother, your unconditional love, sensitivity, patience, attunement, attentiveness, and caring are very much a part of who I am.

To my brother, Ned, a child prodigy, a polymath who was so bored in school that, at age twelve, he built a model nuclear reactor, wrote a speech entitled "peaceful uses of atomic energy" for Chicago's first science fair at the museum, won a first-place ribbon, and was accepted to college at age fourteen, thank you for being such a wonderful inspiration. Ned

ACKNOWLEDGEMENTS

was almost always reading, even while eating. He was a gifted writer and spoke well. It all helped him as he argued cases in city and state supreme courts and wrote briefs for state and federal judges.

My brother would get bored because everything came so easily to him. While practicing law, he would take classes in math, physics, and literature at The University of Chicago. He took a leave of absence from his law practice to get a master's degree in taxation. Later, while still practicing and in his fifties, he entered medical school.

Ned was most influential in his support of me and by his example of academic success and intellectual drive and curiosity. Additionally, my brother was a great teacher. He had a gift of taking any concept and clearly explaining it. I recall dozens of immigrant children coming to our house, and my brother teaching them to read, write, and do math. Several months before he died, he set up shop in a public library and began tutoring children and adults. At his funeral service, there were dozens of people in attendance who he had tutored as young immigrant children. Many of them had become successful professionals.

To my grandchildren, Zachary, Jordyn, Ari, and Alex, let me just say that I am always unbelievably excited just to be with you. You are each so special to me and are filled with joie de vivre. All of you are so happy, energetic, funny, smart, creative, curious, alert, respectful, kind, caring, and most loveable. Thank you for the untold joy you bring me just by being with you.

To my brothers-in-law, Ron and Jerry Feigen, I have known you, respectively, since you were twelve and seventeen years-old. I have seen you both grow and become most outstanding, successful professionals. I value being able to call you family. You both have provided me unmatched software and hardware consultation. My computer doctors even make virtual and in-person house calls. Your vigilance in protecting my files, Jerry, especially while I was writing my book, is most appreciated.

To my sons-in-law, Adam Kramer and Olivier Rubel, you have enriched our family with your high professional successes. Above all, you are amazing and loving parents and husbands. I am happy we are family.

To Jason Kerman, Mara's partner, you are an extremely caring, kind, and most hard-working person. Your recent managerial promotion as assistant general manager is recognition of your skills and trustworthiness.

To Kyle Fager, you are a most consummate editor. From the outset, you skillfully identified the strengths and weaknesses of my manuscript. You then gave me a road map of what to focus on and what to set aside. Throughout the past several years, your suggestions and edits have continuously served to enhance both the clarity of my purpose to help parents and children as well as adding more of my own voice. I thank you for your support, ability to listen and understand what I was trying to say, your penchant for subtle, nuanced changes, and your attention to detail. It has been a pleasure working with you. I could not have done it without you.

To Anna Hall, you are a most gifted book designer. Your beautiful cover illustration captures the essence of my project to raise children to thrive through close connection and contact

ACKNOWLEDGEMENTS

with their parents. Thank you for your artistic talent and contributions both outside and inside the book.

To Jennifer McDonald, my instructor in The Writer's Studio at The University of Chicago, you were instrumental in helping me to write this book. It was for your assignment to write an introduction for our book or short story that I penned both the epilogue and one sentence of my introduction. At the time, I had no clear idea of any content for my project. Thank you for inspiring me to write.

To Mark Hass, journalism professor and also professor in the business school at ASU and former newspaper editor, thank you for being the first person to read, review, and critique my initial manuscript several years ago. Your comments were valid, and you helped me to find an editor and make significant changes to my first draft.

I want to thank my professors at Oberlin College in French studies. Mr. Simon Barenbaum and Mr. Mathis Szykowski, who introduced me to Camus, Sartre, Stendhal, Moliere, and others. In Paris, I had the good fortune of studying with Madeleine Hours at the Louvre. She was *conservateur des musées nationaux* and the first to X-ray and study the painted-over paintings of grand masters. Additionally, her experiential approach in her class was to sit on the floor of the grand gallery on the day the museum was closed to the public and just observe paintings. We would also take field trips and, for example, have lunch at a restaurant while looking out the window and observing the same view Cézanne had while painting a particular mountain. My study of French language and literature was also enhanced by having the opportunity to study at Paris-Sorbonne University and *l'ancienne faculté des lettres d'Aix et les études régionales* in the rural countryside while living with a local family.

I especially want to thank Professors John Thompson and Warren Taylor. Dr. Thompson was one of the main reasons I majored in psychology. He left his clinical practice to teach at Oberlin. I still remember his seminar entitled psychopathology in literature, which took place in his home. And Dr. Taylor, my humanities professor, introduced me to the classics as well as cross-cultural studies. I would drop by his office on the way to the library to discuss my poetry submissions to the Plum Creek review or get inspired by his reciting, from memory, various scenes of Shakespeare's plays, often while standing and acting the part. I still remember him saying, "Mr. Ruff, you see that pile of papers on my desk? The students are not writing about humanity; they are writing about themselves."

I want to thank the Oberlin Musical Union, who gave me the opportunity to sing the Bach's Mass in B Minor with the Oberlin Orchestra, professional soloists, and under the baton of Robert Shaw. It was the most exhilarating, moving, and inspirational creative and artistic experience in my life.

I owe much gratitude to Dr. Alexy Shukin. As one of several first-generation psychologists trained by Carl Rogers, Dr. Shukin's impact on me professionally and personally was significant. In my two-year master's degree program, we studied, wrote about, taught, and trained in the counseling center under Rogers' core concept of empathy. That concept was transformative.

I want to thank Dr. Harris Berenbaum, director and clinical supervisor in my doctoral program at Illinois Institute

ACKNOWLEDGEMENTS

of Technology. Your intensive supervision and support were instrumental in laying a solid groundwork for my practice as a clinical psychologist.

A heartfelt thank you to Dr. Gail Roid, esteemed author of seven published tests, including the *Stanford-Binet Intelligence Scales* (5th and forthcoming 6th Editions), nine books, thirty chapters, and many research journal articles. Dr. Roid is a former professor at Vanderbilt and has made profound contributions to the field of psychological assessments and special education. I value our past professional associations in doing research together toward standardizing my test battery for children in the schools. I am grateful for you serving as the keynote speaker at my interdisciplinary seminar on childhood trauma for county court judges, prosecutors, defense attorneys, probation officers, and department of child services case workers. Thank you for your kind review and favorable endorsement of my book. It means a lot to me.

Laurie and Dave Burns, you are dear friends. I want you to know that your most genuine support and concern really mattered. Thank you for caring and always asking me about how my book was going and showing interest in both me and the subject. You have been my best fans. I appreciate you both.

The city in which I was raised, East Chicago, Indiana, offered me a basic education and foundation in getting along with people from different cultures, races, economic status, and vocational and educational backgrounds. I didn't realize until I got older that such an enriching and diverse assimilation with other people's ways of living served as my initial and intensive psychological internship. They prepared me well not just for my future occupation but for becoming more sensitive and understanding of people.

These past five years have been very personally enriching. After retiring following five decades of intensive, therapeutic, interpersonal relationships with people, I delved into professional literature. I had ample time to visit the ASU library, take out about two hundred books, and read over a thousand journal articles. This was like working on a post-practice dissertation. When I first endeavored in my doctoral dissertation, it was an intensive academic project based on minimal professional experiences. This time, it was the other way around. I had the opportunity to superimpose extensive, interdisciplinary, pioneering research upon all of my years of clinical, practical, and lived experiences. It was most exciting and personally rewarding to superimpose and synthesize state-of-the-art research and revolutionary findings in early child development and neuroscience upon my own best practice and evidence-based models of treatment. I was excited to again have the time to read and discover my field and gain new knowledge. It was also very humbling. In Einstein's words, "The more I learn, the more I realize how much I don't know."

My goal has been to use the many positive relationships I have had the good fortune of enjoying, along with my educational and life experiences, to help repair the world in some small way while adding to the common good. Helping others to ease their pain and to become healthier, happier, more fully functioning children, adolescents, and adults has been a privilege and source of much satisfaction.

ACKNOWLEDGEMENTS:

My strength throughout that journey has always been my family and my children. There is a tribe in Africa called Masai, whose traditional greeting to each other is, *"Casserian Engeri."* It means, "And how are the children?" They do not ask each other, "How are you?" or "How's your day?" but rather, they ask about the next generation.

Finally, I want to thank my thousands of patients of all ages and from all walks of life and in multiple treatment settings over the course of five decades. You came to me as total strangers and entrusted me with your pain, suffering, confusion, and deepest emotions and secrets. I strived to feel your pain and to genuinely see the world from your own perspective. I was always happy to see you grow and lead more normal lives. I did not realize, however, until these later years, with the benefit of physical and emotional distance, time, and age, that I too grew during our time together. Within our meetings, I also became more whole. I know now, going to those tens of thousands of hours of such dialogue, that it is only through such genuine, mutual, intersubjective encounters that we humans become more self-fulfilled, congruent, whole, and alive.

TABLE OF CONTENTS

Acknowledgments VII
Epigraph 1
Introduction 3

Part I: Core Concepts and Inherent Psychological Resources

Chapter 1	Affect Hunger 9
Chapter 2	Conscience 31
Chapter 3	Empathy 47
Chapter 4	Play 63
Chapter 5	Stimulation 77
Chapter 6	Responsive, Sensitive Parenting 91

Part II: Intersubjectivity

Chapter 7	Intersubjectivity-Overview 125
Chapter 8	Psychology and Intersubjectivity 129
Chapter 9	Neuroscience and Intersubjectivity 149
Chapter 10	Intersubjectivity and Psychic Pain 173
Chapter 11	Hands-on Parenting 199
Chapter 12	Conclusions 205

Endnotes 215

"The way in which each human infant is transformed into the finished adult, into the complicated individual version of his city and century, is one of the most fascinating studies open to the curious mind."

— Margaret Mead, *Growing Up in New Guinea*

Introduction

*"I did then what I knew how to do.
Now that I know better, I do better."*
— MAYA ANGELOU

IN EARLY SEPTEMBER 1963, I sat in a small, older classroom at Oberlin College in Ohio nervously waiting for my professor to arrive. Motivation and Emotion was my first freshman class *and* my first course in psychology. Professor John Thompson, with his impressive professional demeanor, arrived impeccably dressed in a dark suit and tie. He walked straight to the lectern, placed a folder on the slanted top, and opened it. Sitting close to him in the front row, I noticed that his lecture was typed. I still recall his first words.

"There's nothing new under the sun in psychology," he told us. "The Greek philosophers said it all centuries ago."

Throughout my fifty years of practice I would think about Dr. Thompson's opening remark, often asking myself, "Is this still true?" It was as if I, a subject of one, was testing a hypothesis. I felt compelled to determine whether current advancements in my chosen field would change the answer. Was my discipline rooted in philosophy, or was it actual science? The question left me uneasy, for I wanted to be able to answer unequivocally that it belonged to the latter.

Now, sixty years later, I believe that Dr. Thompson's initial assertion is no longer true. Intersubjectivity and neuroscience have replaced the centuries-long adherence to Greek philosophy. The enduring belief in the Cartesian self, which is solipsistic and cannot know other minds, has been dispelled. Thanks to neuroscience, psychology's zeitgeist today proposes a self that is born in intersubjectivity. We can infer and understand other people's mental states to predict their behavior, and through brain mapping, neuroscience reveals that we emotionally feel the pain and minds of others. We humans connect with other humans and share emotional experiences.

Parenting a psychologically healthy child is an arduous process—the most difficult human endeavor, in fact—and requires all of our resources. We must be constantly attentive to our helpless newborn, and the job continues into infancy and early childhood. Yet most mothers and fathers parent with little or no guidance. Indeed, most of us parent the same way we were parented. When the warning lights on the dashboard flash red, we can't reach for an owner's manual, and when we get lost, we can't consult a map, turn on the GPS, or print out directions.

I've written this book to help parents understand children's needs and how to meet them. It's aimed at the multitude of well-meaning, loving parents who have nowhere to turn for help, and it's couched within a framework of positive social and emotional development. Even in utero, we possess a need to engage with others as an intersubjective self. As infants, we're prewired to satiate our hunger for "affect," which in psychology means the experience of feeling or emotion. This permits acceptance and confirmation of our humanness. It also provides vital emotional stimulation and the initial attachment bond. Our mother is our first companion. With her and others, we constantly seek emotional responsiveness and sharing, interaction, connection, inclusion, and intimacy. My work focuses on how this process occurs. I offer a best-practice model of parenting based on new scientific evidence and my own evidence-based clinical practice.

I don't write about psychopathology, aberrant behavior, or mental illness. Rather, I provide information intended to help parents and caregivers handle the challenging responsibility of raising children. I focus on what should occur between child and parent to maximize the child's capacity for healthy psychosocial, emotional, and cognitive development. I discuss the requisite psychological resources, which are transferred to the infant as the product of a mutual, bilateral, intersubjective attachment bond between parent and child. This serves as the infant's initial, quintessential intersubjective and emotional foundation, upon which all future social, emotional, and cognitive experiences will be built.

I spent five decades helping children, adolescents, and adults recover from acute parental neglect, deprivation, toxic environmental stress, and trauma. As a result, I gained meaningful insights into what causes poor psychological development and a good understanding of the vital components inherent in the personality makeup of socially and emotionally healthy individuals. The Science of Neglect, as it's called, reveals the deleterious effects of depriving a child's innate hunger for affect, parental love, and protection.

Unfortunately, I've too often struggled to remediate the negative effects of neglect or physical, sexual, or psychological trauma. In many cases, the damage was too severe; the parents and caregivers had failed to satiate the child's innate hunger for affect during the earliest and formative years. Not surprisingly, neglect is the most prevalent form of child abuse, yet it's the least understood and most frequently undiagnosed and untreated. Neglectful parenting and caregiving can cause severe and permanent damage to a child's psychological and cognitive development.

When children are raised by responsive, sensitive parents, they're more likely to thrive. Moreover, they're significantly more resilient and thus are more capable of responding to various stressors throughout life. They're also less likely to develop mental illness and other disorders. Responsive, sensitive parenting and the fulfillment of a child's innate need to satiate affect hunger should be a birthright. Consider this book my contribution toward such a reality.

In the following chapters, I present three central concepts: affect hunger; responsive, sensitive parenting; and

INTRODUCTION

intersubjectivity. Additionally, I discuss four inherent psychological resources necessary for healthy child development. My goal throughout, to paraphrase Maya Angelou, is to help parents "know better and do better." In the interest of client confidentiality and patient privacy, I have changed the names and identifying details that appear in every anecdote of this book.

CHAPTER 1

Affect Hunger

JOHNNY WAS NINE-AND-A-HALF years old when he was admitted to the children's unit of the long-term residential treatment center where I served as clinical director. Like our other young patients, he had suffered trauma and severe neglect. He had been physically abused, and his mother had been seldom present during his infancy and childhood. He had attempted suicide and often experienced defiance and overwhelming rage. During one such fit of rage, he had burned down his family's house. While admitting him, we diagnosed him with major depression with suicidal ideations, post-traumatic stress disorder (PTSD), antisocial behavior, and learning disorders.

The course of treatment for Johnny included intensive group counseling, medication, school, recreational therapy, individual therapy, and family reunification. Prior to his discharge at the age of twelve, I conducted a psychological evaluation. All of Johnny's initial presenting disorders and problems appeared to be in remission. I noted no major depression or PTSD. Johnny was no longer suicidal. He was pleasant, emotive, and sociable and laughed during our interview. Moreover, his IQ of eighty, assessed three years prior, had improved to ninety-eight. He was the perfect example of a child who had experienced toxic environmental stress but had benefited from intensive treatment interventions and intellectual and social stimulation. Before treatment, such children are often tagged with the description "failure to thrive." But if given the basic components of affection, security, safety, and nurturance within a supportive environment of secure attachments, they can thrive.

Johnny's case illustrates a child's resilience and capacity to overcome social, emotional, and intellectual deficiencies without a maternal attachment bond. It also calls into doubt British psychologist John Bowlby's contention that a child's mother, as primary caregiver, must be present on a continuous basis throughout the first two years of a child's life. Based on my own professional experiences, I've found that, in the absence of a full-time mother, alternate caregivers can provide the requisite needs. Thus fathers, older adult siblings, grandparents, relatives, or foster parents can serve as primary guardians or parents.

Central to a child's wellbeing is the emotional need for affection. A newborn innately craves nurturance. We call this affect hunger: emotional hunger for maternal love and the feelings of protection and care implied in the mother-child relationship. Unfortunately, too many infants don't receive the emotional "nutrients" essential for early survival and healthy emotional development. Suffering maternal rejection and being deprived of a mother's love and protection harms a child's capacity

CHAPTER 1: AFFECT HUNGER

to feel secure and to successfully meet later developmental milestones.

Affect hunger is the cosmic glue that binds the newborn to their mother. It is the dark, invisible matter that anchors, guides, and warmly welcomes the infant into the world. The infant possesses an innate need to experience feelings and emotions at birth. Like a plant that bends toward light, infants and children are hardwired to connect with their birth mother. Such a drive originates in the most primitive part of the mammalian brain and is all about survival. Yet this essential psychological need is frequently neglected by parents and caregivers. If the child's persistent affect hunger is not satiated, feelings of emotional deprivation occur. Being loved, protected, and cared for should be a birthright, but many children's basic needs go unmet.

I first became interested in affect hunger after studying the Rorschach Test and learning the Beck method of scoring and interpretation. Throughout my practice, especially regarding differential diagnoses, I have referred to Dr. Samuel J. Beck's description of "The texture determinant, T," which he explores in his book, *Rorschach's Test, II: A Variety of Personality Pictures*[1]:

[The texture determinant, T.] offers a clue to the concept of affect-hunger, projecting an erotic need deeply embedded in the early character formation. D. M. Levy[2] *discusses this concept in relation to maternal overprotection. Some early experimental studies by Levy*[3] *provide controlled observation of this phenomenon and its implication for oral erotic gratification. Relevant to this topic are Harlow's research*[4] *concerning the effects upon*

love in the infant monkey and his use of cloth and wire as mother surrogates. His results appear to point to the importance of close bodily contact.

The experience inherent in texture (T) is one of direct contact and in which the skin feels directly. Thus, T is generic to basic feelings of security, the anxiety aroused owing to deprivation of this contact and the defensive strategies which are activated. The feeling tone projected is related to passive, dependent longings deeply seated in the oral character structure, concomitant with sensed rejection and deprivation, trophic and emotional. The need or "press" projected in T stems from the very roots of the early symbiotic mother-child relationship, so well described by Mahler.

In other words, early in an infant's life, physical contact between infant and caregiver is crucial for laying down a basic sense of security at a time when the child is not yet able to articulate and express his or her own needs.

David Levy, MD, a leading child psychiatrist and advocate of the Rorschach test, wrote a classic paper in 1937 entitled, "Primary Affect Hunger." He interpreted this lack of texture and bodily contact as follows:

The term, affect hunger, is used to mean an emotional hunger for maternal love and those other feelings of protection and care implied in the mother-child relationship. The term has been utilized to indicate a state of privation due primarily to a lack of maternal affection, with a resulting need, as of food in a state of starvation....

CHAPTER 1: AFFECT HUNGER

I am using the term to apply only to individuals who have suffered lack of maternal love in the early years of life. Assuming for the moment the value of maternal love as an essential component in the development of the emotional life, what happens when this element is left out of the primary social relationship? Is it possible that there results a deficiency disease of the emotional life, comparable to a deficiency of vital nutritional elements within the developing organism?[5]

Throughout my years of practice, I have found, in every case in which I conducted a comprehensive psychological evaluation, a consistently high correlation, as well, with affect hunger, maternal rejection, and lack of close bodily contact occurring in the early years of life. This has also been the case with adults who I evaluated and treated, whose problems likely had their origins in primary affect hunger. These adults were physically and emotionally neglected by their parents at an early age. Essentially, they had been deprived and emotionally had become failure-to-thrive children.

Beck, who also spoke of the anxiety triggered when we're deprived of affection and security, first published his book in 1945. Since then, few have followed in his footsteps. While searching the American Psychological Association (APA) databases seventy-one years later, I found only three articles pertaining to affect hunger. Why have so few focused on this critical human need? Is my field ignoring the "God particle," the core ingredient upon which healthy psychological growth depends? Unless this unseen, basic need is met, mother and child fail to bond. Without this spark, our child's emotional life can't ignite, which significantly decreases their ability to thrive.

Current professional thinking and guidelines have changed regarding the meaning of child neglect. The DSM (*Diagnostic and Statistical Manual of Mental Disorders*, Fifth Edition) defines child neglect, in the section entitled "Child Maltreatment and Neglect Problems," as follows:

> *Child Neglect is defined as any confirmed or suspected egregious act or omission by a child's parent or other caregiver that deprives the child of basic age-appropriate needs and thereby results, or has reasonable potential to result, in physical or psychological harm to the child. Child neglect encompasses abandonment; lack of appropriate supervision; failure to attend to necessary emotional or psychological needs; and failure to provide necessary education, medical care, nourishment, shelter, and/or clothing.*[6]

There's a reason why failing to provide our child with warmth, protection, and caring constitutes neglect. Such basic needs must be met to sustain healthy psychological functioning. They provide the building blocks for all future psychosocial and emotional development. They are the psychological equivalent of oxygen and food, which we crave from birth and require throughout our lives. If our affect hunger is met, we will gain a greater capacity to regulate our lives while seeking meaning and self-fulfillment and becoming more self-sufficient. The hunger, though, will never cease.

As already mentioned, there is little to be found in professional literature and research relevant to affect hunger.

CHAPTER 1: AFFECT HUNGER

However, one psychologist, Dr. Bryan Egeland at the University of Minnesota, became a pioneer in the study of neglect. In 1975, he began a research study and followed two hundred children from birth to adolescence. His goal was to discover the causal influences and effects of child abuse and neglect. His classic study resulted in several salient findings:

1. As many as fifty-five percent of the two hundred subjects did not become securely attached to their mother by the time they were one year old.
2. Children raised by psychologically unavailable mothers were more withdrawn and dependent and experienced the highest degree of decline in mental and behavioral development as they aged. These levels were significantly worse than those of the children who had actually been physically abused.
3. The mothers who hadn't been abused as children were significantly more able to comprehend and respond to their children's emotional needs.
4. The mothers who were extremely needy were unable to nurture. They expected their children to gratify their own needs for love and nurturance.
5. The study concluded that "teaching caretaking skills is far less important than helping these mothers understand the meaning of the child's behavior and how to respond to it."[7]

Child neglect isn't necessarily intentional. But whether or not an emotionally unavailable parent elects to withhold their child's emotional needs, the child's psychological welfare can suffer serious consequences. Neglect is the most widespread form of child maltreatment. A recent study of child neglect and its correlation with violent behavior found that child neglect may be equally or more predictive of physical violence in adulthood than physical abuse. Such a finding challenges the "cycle of violence" theory.

Tactile

The core attribute associated with affect hunger, touch is the infant's primary craving for both survival and comfort. Tactile stimulation is the infant's first language. The qualitative and quantitative nature of that felt communication represents the primary source of warmth, safety, nurturance, and love for the infant.

Researchers in child development have significantly minimized the role of touch and tactile stimulation. Psychologist Harry Harlow studied the effects of touch versus deprivation in primates at the University of Wisconsin in the 1950s. Researchers observed rhesus monkeys and surrogate mothers for several years. Analysis of the data indicated the following:

> *Characteristics of mothers, other than as food resources, are important for attachment. When presented with a wire surrogate where milk could be obtained and with a terry cloth mother without milk, infants spent most of their time with the terry cloth surrogate. When the infants were placed in a novel environment or threatened with a strange object, these monkeys seemed to derive comfort from the cloth surrogate. Concluded that this*

CHAPTER 1: AFFECT HUNGER

effect could not be explained by secondary reinforcement from feeding and that other biological drives must make contact comfort reinforcing. The data obtained makes it obvious that contact comfort is a variable of overwhelming importance in the development of affectional responses, whereas lactation is a variable of negligible importance.[8]

Harlow's findings contributed significantly to understanding the critical nature of caregiving and companionship in psychosocial development. In essence, experimental findings supported the hypothesis that the mother-infant bond is not primarily associated with satiating physiological needs but with satisfying emotional needs for acceptance, love, and affection.

Harlow's concept of "contact comfort" was expanded into one of the most significant psychological theories of social development of the twentieth century.

John Bowlby, psychologist and psychoanalyst, is best known for formulating Attachment Theory. He based his hypotheses on evolutionary theory and believed that children are genetically and biologically "pre-programmed" to survive. His basic tenets are as follows:

1. A child has an innate (i.e. inborn) need to attach to one main attachment figure (i.e. monotropy). Bowlby advocated that there should be one main and most important figure upon whom the child bonds (typically the mother). Bowlby saw this maternal attachment as unique and unlike any other future attachments.

Additionally, Bowlby formulated that a lack of maternal attachment results in "serious negative consequences," possibly even "affectionless psychopathy." His conceptualization of one primary maternal bond resulted in his theory of "maternal deprivation."
2. A child should receive the continuous care of this singlemost attachment figure for approximately the first two years of life.
3. The long-term consequences of maternal deprivation might include the following:
    - Delinquency
    - Reduced intelligence
    - Increased aggression
    - Depression
    - Affectionless psychopathy
4. Short-term separation from an attachment leads to distress.
5. The child's attachment relationship with their primary caregiver leads to the development of an internal working model.[9]

Bowlby's Theory of Attachment asserts that infants are born programmed to seek connection and proximity to their caretakers for the sake of survival, creating a close **attachment bond**. Over time, children internalize this attachment process and use these base relationships to form a prototype for later relationships outside the family. This relationship prototype is a set of archetypes of themselves and others called the **internal working models** (IWMs).

CHAPTER 1: AFFECT HUNGER

Bowlby's theory embodies the insight that attachment is critical in parenting. Successful emotional bonding significantly increases the chances of normal psychosocial growth. If the mother-child bond is disrupted in the early stages, there is a high risk for emotional problems, poor social adjustment, antisocial behavior, and juvenile delinquency.

John Bowlby's Attachment Theory is one of the major contributions in the field of psychology, but it's not without criticism, especially his concept of maternal deprivation. Bowlby asserted that the maternal attachment is both unique and the strongest. The research of Rudolph Schaffer and Peggy Emerson[10] indicates that, from eight months to eighteen months, only thirteen percent of babies maintained an attachment to only one person. Some babies had as many as five attachments. Another criticism of Bowlby is that he doesn't differentiate between deprivation (the loss of or damage to attachment) and privation (the failure to develop attachment).

Child psychiatrist Michael Rutter emphasizes that "the quality of attachment bond is the most important factor, rather than just deprivation during the critical period." In his book, *Maternal Deprivation Reassessed*,[11] Rutter notes that privation and deprivation affect children differently. Specifically, a child who experiences privation exhibits "clinging, dependent behavior, attention-seeking, and indiscriminate friendliness." As the child ages, he has difficulty in following rules and doesn't experience a sense of guilt for disruptive behaviors. Rutter's research showed a high incidence of antisocial behavior, affectionless psychopathy, disorders of language, and delayed cognitive development and physical growth among youngsters who suffered privation.

Rutter concluded that the severe problems reported in his research don't occur merely due to the lack of a maternal attachment bond, as stated by Bowlby. Rather, the child suffered a lack of intellectual stimulation and socialization because of the lack of an attachment figure in general. Furthermore, Rutter contends that such privation-induced problems and deficits are reversible; they can be remediated with proper treatment interventions.[12]

A fulfilled, happy, and healthy mother is preferable to an unhappy, miserable, or depressed mother who is present on a continuous basis. In fact, less interaction with the latter is in the child's best interest.

Since touch is a child's first language, it's the primary means by which the newborn and developing infant receives stimulation. As already discussed, a direct association exists between sensory deprivation and developmental delay. Healthy emotional and social growth depend on mechanosensory stimulation, which is vital across all organisms.

Hopper and Pinneau conducted research on orphans in Eastern European institutions.[13] Having suffered severe neglect and emotional deprivation, the children were diagnosed with attachment disorders and impaired levels of emotional, social, and cognitive functioning. They also suffered from a high number of acute infections. The researchers found a significant reduction in regurgitation as a result of being held for just ten additional minutes per day. L. Casler, one of the authors of the study, found that children who received an additional twenty minutes of tactile stimulation per day scored higher on developmental measurement scales.

CHAPTER 1: AFFECT HUNGER

Touch is life altering—psychologically and physiologically. Dong Liu (2000) and a team of researchers studied the effects of maternal licking on rat pups.[14] They measured changes in gene expression in the part of the brain that regulates behavioral and endocrine response to stress. In another study, deprived worms responded favorably to taps, and the changes could be measured on the molecular level.[15]

In addition to children, monkeys, rats, and worms, adults benefit from touch. Researchers Steven Cady and Gwen Jones found that chair massages lowered employees' blood pressure and anxiety in the workplace and increased their speed and accuracy on math problems.[16] Patients suffering from burns and eating disorders were found to have lower stress levels, anxiety, and clinical symptoms after massage therapy.[17] HIV-positive men who received daily massages showed an increased number of immune cells.[18]

The Science of Neglect
Neglect is the most prevalent form of child maltreatment at 78%. The second most? Physical abuse at 18%. Many of the children, adolescents, and adults that I treated would tell me they would rather have been beaten with a belt than neglected and rejected by their parents.

What psychological impact does neglect have on children? How does it affect their social, emotional, and cognitive development?

Definitions

According to the APA's online dictionary of psychology, parental neglect can be defined as follows:

The denial of attention, care, or affection considered essential for the normal development of a child's physical, emotional, and intellectual qualities, usually due to indifference from, disregard by, or impairment in the child's caregivers.

The APA defines parental rejection thus:

Persistent denial of approval, affection, or care of a child by one or both parents, sometimes concealed beneath a cover of overindulgence or overprotection. The frequent results are corrosion of the child's self-esteem and self-confidence, a poor self-image, inability to form attachments to others, tantrums, generalized hostility, and development of psychophysical and emotional disturbances.[19]

Not surprisingly, my patients who had been assessed with mood disorders or other severe clinical disorders reported affect hunger most consistently as a psychological need. In almost all cases, the high incidence of measured affect hunger was associated with documented longstanding parental neglect or rejection. Recall what Samuel Beck wrote regarding the "T" response as a determinant of affect hunger:

The feeling tone projected is related to passive, dependent longings deeply-seated in the oral character structure, concomitant with sensed rejection and deprivation, trophic and emotional.

Essential Findings and the Case of Gladys

Harvard University's Center on the Developing Child summed up the essential findings of recent scientific publications and presentations as follows:

> *Building the foundations of successful development in childhood requires responsive relationships and supportive environments. Beginning shortly after birth, the typical "serve and return" interactions that occur between young children and the adults who care for them actually affect the formation of neural connections and the circuitry of the developing brain. Over the next few months, as babies reach out for greater engagement through cooing, crying, and making facial expressions—and adults "return the serve" by responding with similar vocalizing and expressiveness—these reciprocal and dynamic exchanges literally shape the architecture of the developing brain.*
>
> *Because responsive relationships are both expected and essential, their absence is a serious threat to a child's development and wellbeing. Sensing a threat activates biological stress response systems, and excessive activation of those systems can render a toxic effect on developing brain circuitry. When the lack of responsiveness persists, the adverse effects of toxic stress can compound the lost opportunities for development associated with limited or ineffective interaction.*
>
> *Chronic neglect is associated with a wider range of damage than active abuse, but it receives less attention in policy and*

practice. Science tells us that young children who experience significantly limited caregiver responsiveness may sustain a range of adverse physical and mental health consequences that actually produce more widespread developmental impairments than overt physical abuse. These can include cognitive delays, stunting of physical growth, impairments in executive function and self-regulation skills, and disruptions of the body's stress response.

Studies on children in a variety of settings show conclusively that severe deprivation or neglect:

- *disrupts the ways in which children's brains develop and process information, thereby increasing the risk for attentional, emotional, cognitive, and behavioral disorders*
- *alters the development of biological stress response systems, leading to greater risk for anxiety, depression, cardiovascular problems, and other chronic health impairments later in life*
- *is associated with significant risk for emotional and interpersonal difficulties, including high levels of negativity, poor impulse control, and personality disorders, as well as low levels of enthusiasm, confidence, and assertiveness*
- *is associated with significant risk for learning difficulties and poor school achievement, including deficits in executive function and attention regulation, low IQ scores, poor reading skills, and low rates of high school graduation*

CHAPTER 1: AFFECT HUNGER

> *The negative consequences of deprivation and neglect can be reversed or reduced through appropriate and timely interventions, but merely removing a young child from an insufficiently responsive environment does not guarantee positive outcomes. Children who experience severe deprivation typically need therapeutic intervention and highly supportive care to mitigate the adverse effects and facilitate recovery.*[20]

There are cases, however, in which the early privation and trauma are so devastating that remediations, intensive or otherwise, don't alter the severe disorders and psychopathology. Some individuals' levels of functioning and stages of development are so arrested and damaged that even habilitation is improbable. Gladys is an example of such a child, but her story shows that with sensitive treatment which incorporates these insights, the improbable can actually be possible.

I met Gladys when she was eight years old and at a residential treatment center (RTC), just after I graduated from college. I was a residential technician working the midnight shift. My main responsibility was to wake the children in the morning, help them get ready for the day, and take them to breakfast and then school. Gladys had never attended school. She had been removed from her home by the Department of Child Services (DCS) due to charges of severe physical, sexual, and emotional abuse. Gladys had essentially served as her father's slave. She was chained to her bed during the day while her father was at work. When he returned home, she made him dinner.

Not long after she was in our care, I entered Gladys's room one morning to wake her and take her to our in-house school for the first time. She was sound asleep, so I tapped on her shoulder. She awoke startled and angry and lunged at me, scratching my face and tearing my polo shirt. Fortunately, we were able to work through the crisis, and after Gladys settled down, I walked her into a classroom for the first time in her life.

Twelve years later, I was having lunch in the staff cafeteria of a psychiatric hospital. Among the people sitting at my table was a clinical social worker.

"Hi," she said. "I'm Sandy. I'm new on the staff."

After exchanging pleasantries, we spoke about Sandy's previous job.

"I worked at the state psychiatric hospital," she said. "My final assignment before leaving the hospital was to fly with a nineteen-year-old female patient to Florida for placement in an adult group home. She was in the state mental health system for most of her life. She was hospitalized for several years at a residential treatment center after her father enslaved her."

I knew right away who she was talking about. "Is her name Gladys?"

Sandy gasped. She caught her breath and stared at me in disbelief. "How did you know?"

"I was her counselor at her first residential treatment center eleven years ago."

"She's gone from one treatment setting to another her entire life," Sandy replied with a nod. "She's the angriest and saddest child I've ever known. She left that initial RTC where you met her when she was ten and lived with an aunt. Because of her poor conduct, educational deficits, and depression, she went to a special education school. Her Aunt Alice really tried to show her love. She fixed up her married daughter's former bedroom and let Gladys pick out the color of the paint, bedding, and new carpet. For her first Christmas, Alice surprised Gladys with a puppy. She named her dog Cuddles. Gladys really took care of that dog. I think that she felt safe with it.

"After about a year at her aunt's, Gladys made a serious suicide attempt. She overdosed on street drugs and was in the ICU for days. After that, she was placed in a long-term RTC for three years. She did pretty well and was discharged to her first therapeutic foster home when she was thirteen. Throughout adolescence, she made two other suicide attempts, was expelled from school for beating up a student, and ran away with a twenty-year-old man. She was court-ordered at fifteen to remain in an RTC until they determined she wasn't a danger to herself or others. She was finally placed in a therapeutic group home out of state. She loves animals and has always wanted to be a veterinarian, so I helped find her this group home in Florida that's near a zoo. She's enrolled in a training program to become a zookeeper. I also spoke to the local welfare department. They're going to get Gladys a service dog."

Four years after talking with Sandy, I received the following email:

Hello Dr. Ruff,
 I am forwarding you this email I just received from Gladys. I think you would be interested in reading it.

Dear Ms. Sandy,

I haven't talked with you in a long while, but I remember you told me I could write you anytime.

Since you brought me to Florida four years ago, a lot of things have happened to me. I stayed in the adult therapeutic group home for three years. During that time, I became a certified zookeeper. As you know, I love animals. I have been working at the county zoo steady for the past two years.

About a year ago, I met Alejandro. He is Cuban. We both speak Spanish together. He has a good job as a union construction worker. His whole family came to America before he was born.

I left the group home just before last Christmas. Alejandro and I moved into a two-bedroom patio home, and Cuddles (number two) also lives with us. I still take Prozac, but I don't have thoughts to hurt myself. I go to an outpatient support group once a week.

The best thing is that I know Alejandro loves me and I trust he won't hurt me. His parents and brothers and sisters also care about me. His sisters and brothers call me "little sis," and his mother says I am her child too. They call me a lot, and we visit them all the time and celebrate holidays and birthdays together. I never had a family before. I never had a chance to just be a child. I didn't have a mother, and my father molested and abused me. I was just an object. I now have people who love me and care for me. Alejandro's family gave me my first birthday party ever last month. I am twenty-four now but feel like I am just having my childhood and feel like a real person.

I do not feel all the pain and anger anymore. I know I am a good person and not evil. Alejandro knows all about what

CHAPTER 1: AFFECT HUNGER

happened to me and tells me that he loves me just for who I am.

I am going to start classes at the local community college. I am not sure what I want to be, maybe a medical tech or even a teacher. I learned how to swim and go to the pool a lot and also run. The exercise helps me to relax. I finally sleep good at night and don't have any nightmares or flashbacks.

Alejandro's family is real religious. I never believed in God, but I went to church for the first time last week. I am even thinking I might visit my father in prison.

I hope you are doing good too.

Thank you for helping me and getting me my therapy dog!

Your former patient,

    Gladys

CHAPTER 2

Conscience

> *"I feel within me a peace above all earthly dignities, a still and quiet conscience."*
> — WILLIAM SHAKESPEARE, *HENRY VIII*

A DEPRESSED OR characterologically impaired individual often presents themselves to the public as fulfilled and accomplished while masking their true self. "Richard Cory," a poem by Edward Arlington Robinson (1897), familiar to many thanks to the version from Simon and Garfunkel, captures our inability to glimpse someone's true inner feelings:

Whenever Richard Cory went down town,
We people on the pavement looked at him:
He was a gentleman from sole to crown,
Clean favored, and imperially slim.
And he was always quietly arrayed,
And he was always human when he talked;
But still he fluttered pulses when he said,

"Good-morning," and he glittered when he walked.
And he was rich—yes, richer than a king—
And admirably schooled in every grace:
In fine, we thought that he was everything
To make us wish that we were in his place.
So on we worked, and waited for the light,
And went without the meat, and cursed the bread;
And Richard Cory, one calm summer night,
Went home and put a bullet through his head.

Richard Cory appeared happy, like someone who had it all. Yet inwardly, he was depressed. If Cory was a psychopath, we could add one word to the poem's final line:

Went home and put a bullet through his mother's *head.*

I've witnessed the truth of Robinson's poem first hand, unfortunately, and can attest to the clinical validity of his understanding of human nature. The most severe characterological deficit is the lack of an ingrained conscience—that inner voice and intuitive sense that gauges the morality of our behavior and indicates whether we've successfully adapted to cultural norms. Our conscience serves as our moral compass, helping us function in the world as responsible citizens. Without it, we're less human and more flawed, and pose a risk to ourselves and others.

We can't assess human personality based on outward appearances. To the world, we present a persona. Only to our inner selves do we reveal our true personality. Often, our personality

CHAPTER 2: CONSCIENCE

traits are closely aligned with our outward appearances. Indeed, typically the differences between someone's persona and true self are subtle and nuanced. Only after conducting a thorough, skillful psychological evaluation can we accurately assess and differentially diagnose inherent personality components.

While serving as a consultant to a school district, I was called to the high school to provide grief counseling to students and staff after a high school senior had killed herself at home the previous night. Kay, the student in question, seemingly had everything going for her. She was an honors student, prom queen, and athlete. She came from a loving family and had won a scholarship to a prestigious university. On the night she took her own life, she returned home and removed her cat from the garage. After baking cookies and leaving them on the kitchen table with a note telling her family she loved them, she went into the garage, turned on the car's motor, and died of asphyxiation.

I met with the entire senior class in the gym the morning after. Having consulted with the school and others already, we had a coordinated plan in place among faculty, counselors, social workers, and administrators. We arranged several hundred chairs in groups, and students were free to get up, walk around, and sit in on another group with a different group leader or friends.

Kay's suicide had a profound impact on her classmates. She had touched many of their lives and had been involved in countless activities, and because of her popularity, leadership, and success, her decision to take her own life had shocked everyone. I led several groups and stayed for a final group meeting to close out the day. Unlike at a therapy session, where I would guide the discourse, I served primarily as a facilitator to help students share their feelings. We scheduled follow-up or individual sessions with the school counselors and social workers as needed. Below are some of the students' responses:

I can't believe Kay is gone. Why would she ever do that? She was always smiling and seemed so happy.

She was in most of my classes. She was so kind and helpful to everyone. I secretly wished I could be her. She had it all: honor roll, cheerleader, boyfriend, friends, a great family, and a scholarship to college. It makes no sense.

This may seem weird to say, but maybe it's better to just be average. Kay must have had so much pressure to be perfect and successful and covered it up.

I dated Kay sophomore year. She was the most caring person I ever knew. She would do anything to help anyone. I always think about her. I don't believe she is gone.

The potential risk for some to commit suicide is unpredictable based on outward appearances. The same can be said for murder—something I learned while conducting court-ordered psychological evaluations of many adolescents and adults charged with murder.

Tyra seemed like an average teenager. But one night she lay down in bed next to her mother, waited for her to fall asleep,

CHAPTER 2: CONSCIENCE

and then shot and killed her. A few days later, I was asked by the court to conduct a psychological evaluation of the defendant. Throughout her interview, Tyra was outgoing and socially interactive. She was pleasant and cooperative in responding to interview questions, maintained good eye contact, and frequently smiled. My initial impression was that Tyra's behavior was superficial. I didn't sense genuine affect or emotional connection.

"Tyra," I said at the beginning of the evaluation, "tell me about your relationships."

"I live with my mom and my sister. My relationship with my mother is good."

"How are you feeling now?"

"Okay."

"Do you know why you're here?"

"Yes, for an evaluation."

I discontinued the interview and proceeded with formal psychological testing.

Kay's and Tyra's evaluations proved remarkably similar. In both cases, the individuals impressed others as happy. They smiled and were outgoing, friendly, and socially interactive. Kay was in complete denial of her severe depression, while Tyra was unaware of her homicidal ideations, showed no remorse, and never asked for help. Tyra's behavior was typical for an individual who lacks a conscience. Such individuals possess the ability to disassociate their actions from the nature and outcome of their behavior; they take no responsibility.

An internalized conscience indicates that a child understands norms and societal expectations and intuits which lines not to cross. During moments of doubt, their inner voice whispers or even shouts "No!" to prevent socially unacceptable behavior. The notion of respect for boundaries, law, and the welfare of others is a given. They clearly understand the limits of entitlement and the importance of being a citizen within a community. Socrates referred to this inner mechanism as a "daimonic sign," the "inner fight" or voice that one hears just before making a mistake. Conscience is an essential resource for healthy psychological development. It also bolsters national and international law. Assuming responsibility or maintaining a sense of concern for another person's welfare is a legal matter, not just a moral index of character.

While hearing a murder case, a judge seeks answers to two questions. First, does the defendant know right from wrong? And second, does the accused individual express a sense of remorse for their actions? As an expert witness in various cases, I had a professional responsibility to answer such questions in court.

Unlike depressive disorders, psychopathy and antisocial personality disorders are much less treatable. A combination of therapy and medication typically remediates symptoms of depression. But in the case of a personality-disordered individual, neither medication nor therapy has a high probability of success. Lacking a conscience, such a patient refuses to accept ownership of their deviant behavior. The extreme denial, poor judgment, and lack of boundaries make it difficult to alter such negative attitudes and behaviors. The solution is to habilitate. There's nothing to rehabilitate; the conscience is absent. There's nothing to fix; it never existed. Such a critical component must be internalized at a young age. When that doesn't happen, it's often too late.

Moral Development

Several current scientific studies explore the development of conscience in early childhood. The topic is researched from many different perspectives, including cognition, empathy, moral awareness, emotional understanding, the internalization of rules, and the onset of prosocial behavior. My own survey of current studies indicates that the focus is heavily weighted toward moral development.

A conscience is generally viewed as the sum of the influence of most primary psychological components in early child development, including affective, cognitive, social, and motivational constructs. Rather than focusing on this traditional approach, researchers have recently proposed a newer framework for conducting research on morality. Its perspective differs due to the focus on moral development throughout the lifespan, as opposed to the narrow concentration on early childhood.[21]

Ross A. Thompson, in his research on the development of early childhood conscience, broke from previous theories by suggesting that morality is essentially shaped by a child's fear of parental punishment or rejection for not being good. Until rather recently, the theoretical models of conscience hypothesized that children are egocentric or averse to punishment. In practice and research, people have assumed that children's behavior must be conditioned. Parenting, in other words, has been based on a behavioral reward system that assumes children can be shaped to be obedient. Guilt, meanwhile, is the fear and anxiety of not receiving parental love—or losing it altogether. Many prominent psychologists have espoused such an egocentric conceptualization.

In 2010, Grazyna Kochanska and her colleagues studied the role of familial socialization in a child's adaptive and competent functioning.[22] The sample consisted of one hundred children assessed at twenty-five, thirty-eight, and fifty-two months. Researchers measured two dynamics: children's internalization of their parents' rules, and empathic concern toward each parent. The research findings noted a positive correlation with the child's history of empathy toward the mother and a correlation with future socialization. The authors concluded that the results emphasize "the roles or classic components of morality, moral conduct, affect, and self as antecedents of an adaptive developmental trajectory from toddler to early school age."

Two years later, Marc de Rosnay and Elian Fink conducted a longitudinal study of 115 children ranging between a year old and kindergarten age to assess developmental predictors and behavioral features of children's moral motivation.[23] The key finding was that children's conscience is highly correlated with their empathy and positive social conduct.

Research exists on differing types of moral experiences. Adam Brenner's 2014 study[24] explored an encounter between two mutual subjects (I-Thou) and compared it to a relationship based on the internalization of external norms. The authors concluded that only I-Thou encounters serve to foster the development of moral decisions. Why? Because a person's conscience is based on their genuine concern and moral obligation toward the other person. As such, a conscience exists to "make moral choices to help others" based on mutual recognition, as opposed to merely complying with socially or culturally accepted expectations.

Emotion Regulation

"We can define emotion regulation as follows: the ability to respond with the full range of emotions to the ongoing demands of experience in a manner that is socially tolerable and sufficiently flexible to permit spontaneous reactions, including the ability to delay spontaneous reactions as needed."[25] The lack of an appropriate level of emotion regulation often results in an individual's negative emotional arousal. This significantly diminishes their capacity to socially adapt and behave in an appropriate, socially acceptable manner.

Researchers Martha Bell and Christy Wolfe write:

As is understood, the infant undergoes developmental changes in emotion regulation as he or she moves from a state of complete dependence on caregivers for emotional regulation to becoming more independent and capable and responsible for self-regulation of emotions. Early emotion regulation is primarily a bottom-up process in which the responses of the caregiver influence innate physiological mechanisms. At about three months of age, the infant develops a modicum of voluntary control. And, around the age of twelve months, there is more purposeful control observed coinciding with increasingly developing motor skills and types of behavioral communications.[26]

A strong positive correlation exists between empathic concern and effortful control. Children who demonstrate a high degree of effortful control also have a high degree of empathic concern. Researchers Nancy Eisenberg and Natalie Eggum compared well-regulated children who had effortful control to children who had minimal self-regulation:

Well-regulated children who have control over their ability to focus and shift attention have been found to be relatively prone to sympathy, regardless of their emotional reactivity. This is because they can modulate their negative vicarious emotions to maintain an optimal level of emotional arousal. In contrast, children who are unable to regulate their emotions, especially if they are dispositional or prone to intense negative emotions, are found to be low in dispositional sympathy and prone to personal distress.[27]

Thus, good emotion regulation will enable a child to interact with his or her environment with greater clarity and flexibility, and with better ability to respond to a wide range of circumstances.

The Moral Life of Babies

Researchers conducted a fascinating study at the Yale Infant Cognition Center. The goal was to determine whether three-to-five-month-old babies could tell the difference between right and wrong. For the experiment, infants watched a puppet show. One puppet tried to open a box, and a second puppet slammed the box shut, preventing the first puppet from opening it. When shown the two puppets later, eighty percent of the infants selected the "nice" puppet by reaching for it. Additionally, the infants averaged only five seconds of eye contact with the bad puppet but maintained thirty-three seconds of eye contact with the good puppet. The experiment points to an infant's early sense of morality and strongly suggests an innate, predisposed sense of "good" and "justice."

In his article "The Moral Life of Babies," Paul Bloom dispels the commonly held notion that babies are born, as the philosopher Rousseau said, "perfect idiots . . . knowing nothing." Even Sigmund Freud and Jean Piaget posited that a child is born an amoral animal. "I think one of the great discoveries of modern psychology is that this view of babies is mistaken," Bloom writes. "A growing body of evidence, though, suggests that humans do have a rudimentary moral sense from the very start of life."

Dr. Bloom offers the following key points regarding babies' morality:

- Babies have an actual understanding of mental life.
- Toddlers have a mental model not merely of the world but of the world as understood by someone else.
- Another possibility is that babies do, in fact, use their knowledge from Day 1 not for action but for learning.
- Joseph Heinrich and his colleagues concluded that much of the morality that humans possess is a consequence of the culture in which they are raised, not their innate capacities.
- Babies seem to want to assuage the pain of others. Once they have enough physical competence (starting at about

one year old), they soothe others in distress by stroking and touching or by handing over a bottle or toy.
- Toddlers tend to spontaneously help, even without prompting, encouragement, or reward.
- To have a genuinely moral system, some things have to matter, and what we see in babies is the development of mattering.
- Babies have an overall preference for good actors over bad, but babies are drawn to bad actors when those actors are punishing bad behavior.
- Contemporary researchers in social psychology and social neuroscience have discovered the powerful emotional underpinning of what we once thought of as cool, untroubled, mature moral deliberation.
- Babies' moral experiences are instinctive, just like adults'.
- The aspect of morality that we marvel at—its generality and universality—is the product of culture, not of biology.
- The idea that we're born with a natural disapproval of things like lying, breaking a promise, and murder is a misconception. While we have evolved to disapprove of such things, we can also evolve to approve of things such as kindness to kin.[28]

My Clinical Practice Findings

Most individuals who lack an internalized conscience and the capacity to regulate their emotions have never formed a positive maternal or paternal attachment. The parents of these individuals are typically emotionally and/or physically unavailable. During my fifty years of clinical experience, I sat with thousands of such youngsters in outpatient clinics, inpatient clinics, residential clinics, schools, juvenile detention centers, and prisons. Children classified with antisocial behavioral problems are emotionally detached because they received inadequate nurturance, warmth, safety, and bonding during their formative years. I often sat across from them, looked into their eyes, and felt no emotional interchange or connection.

Almost all individuals who lack an internalized conscience have experienced abuse of some kind, toxic environmental stress, or neglect. Often, children and adolescents with severe behavioral disorders have experienced multiple traumas. Invariably, the parental abuse or toxic stress occurred in the earliest, most vital developmental period: birth to three years of age.

It's not always easy to determine whether a child has the capacity to self-regulate their impulses; some freely choose not to self-regulate. Without a conscience, children tend to be impulsive and shortsighted and often engage in thrill-seeking activities. They like to live for the moment and act on a whim. Their tendencies to act in a rebellious or illegal manner characterize a pattern of negative and hostile behavior. Such a poor level of psychological functioning and symptomology is associated with characterological or dysfunctional behavioral patterns.

Oppositional-defiant or antisocial features are typically associated with a poorly developed conscience. The defiance is demonstrated by disruptive behavioral patterns and defiance of authority both at home and at school. Moreover, children with severe conduct problems struggle and often refuse to accept responsibility for their illegal or disruptive and inappropriate behavior. They tend to project blame for their negative actions onto others. One of the first patients I saw as a psychologist was placed in a diagnostic assessment unit of a state psychiatric hospital after being charged with murder. When I asked this twenty-one-year-old man why he had committed murder, he said, "It was his fault. He shouldn't have been in front of me."

When assessing behavioral problems and antisocial behavior in children and adolescents, we must be thorough and not assume that what we see on the outside is what's going on inside. Depression and suicidal ideations can be masked, either by oppositional-defiant behavior or by the pleasant, well-mannered performance of someone "admirably schooled in every grace." Such psychological defenses hide a patient's true feelings, whether they feel unwanted, unappreciated, or misunderstood or see themselves as socially or physically inadequate. As humans, we can repress our anger and dysphoria or externalize it. And we can avoid close, intersubjective dialogue or human attachments, especially if we don't possess the internal resources to engage others in a normal manner.

The lack of an ingrained conscience, combined with serious behavioral problems, suggests longstanding or pervasive social and emotional delays. A disproportionate gap exists between the child's chronological age and her emotional age, and her arrested development will require intensive therapeutic interventions.

Most of us are familiar with the old saying, oft-repeated by parents and teachers: "He or she is acting out for attention." Sometimes that's true. For children who have been mistreated

CHAPTER 2: CONSCIENCE

and lack responsive parenting and nurturing attachments, misbehaving does gain attention. But often oppositional-defiant or borderline behaviors are at the heart of the problem.

I've conducted approximately eight thousand psychological evaluations and have consistently found two personality features associated with serious diagnostic classifications or diagnoses: psychic pain and affect hunger. It doesn't matter if the diagnosis is at the low or high end of the behavior-disorder or depressive or mood-disorder spectrum. The failure to satiate a child's affect hunger, I believe, results in intolerable pain. People can act out and externalize their pain, anger, and suffering or internalize it. In either case, intolerable emotional pain can cause an individual to harm others or themselves.

Whenever testifying in court as an expert witness regarding an individual I had evaluated, I would first present my findings, prompted by the defendant's attorney. Then I would be examined by the prosecutor. In criminal cases, especially those involving a murder charge, the judge would invariably ask me the same question: "In your opinion, does the defendant know right from wrong?" In most cases, my answer was yes.

CHAPTER 3

Empathy

"Human life and humanity come into being in genuine encounters. The hope for this hour depends upon the renewal of the immediacy of dialogue among human beings."

— Martin Buber

During my master's practicum at the college counseling center, I found my empathy skills tested on a regular basis. One day while reviewing the intake form of my next adult patient, still seated in the waiting room, I noticed he had left the form mostly blank. He had filled out his name—Dale—and had referred to his problem as "serious." That was it.

I fetched Dale and brought him to my office.

After we sat down across from one another, Dale pulled out a gun, set it down on the coffee table next to his chair, and looked at me. "It's loaded."

I felt the muscles in my stomach and then my neck tighten.

Dale stared at me.

I opened my mouth—at first, I think, just to breathe. Then I spoke. "I see you came for a serious problem, Dale. Would you like to tell me about it?"

"Well, I've been having these thoughts of suicide."

"How often?"

"Lately, pretty much all the time. I can't eat or sleep."

"Have you had counseling before?"

"No, but I tried. I'm a Vietnam vet and went to the VA Hospital in Chicago. I filled out papers, and they told me to come back in six months for an appointment. I think I have PTSD. I was a gunnery sergeant in the Marine Corps. Then I started drinking even more. I still do pot."

I spotted the gold band on his left ring finger. "I see you have a wedding ring."

"Yes. Jennie and I got married after we graduated high school and just before I shipped out to Vietnam. We've been together through a lot. I'm afraid I'm letting her and our two sons down. She's working hard as a special-ed teacher, and I'm enrolled here as a full-time student. I have one more year to get my bachelor's."

"Dale," I said, "this is a big step for you to come in today. I can tell you really want help. Would it be okay with you if I called in our counseling center director to discuss some treatment options?"

Dale relaxed his shoulders and leaned back in his chair. "Sure. That'd be fine."

When Dr. Hartford, our director, joined us, I filled him in on Dale's problems. Then I turned to Dale. "I'm recommending that you go to our local hospital nearby. They have an excellent

CHAPTER 3: EMPATHY

adult psychiatric unit. You'd first be evaluated by their staff in the ER. You'd be safe there and can get the help you've wanted for a while now."

"Yes, Mr. Ruff, I'll do that."

With Dale's permission and the advice of our director, we called an ambulance to transport Dale to the hospital. I then asked Dale if I could contact his wife to let her know the situation.

"You'll have to leave your weapon," I said.

He agreed to both.

I waited with Dale and then walked him out to the ambulance.

After the ambulance pulled away, I felt relief for Dale. I'd been determined to let him know that I genuinely cared about him and understood his difficulties. As I returned to the office, I realized that my shirt was soaking wet.

Dale's case is a classic example of Post Traumatic Stress Disorder. It also shows how genuine empathy on the part of the therapist can allow for a potentially volatile situation to be defused so that the client can receive the help he needed.

∾

I've been fortunate to have had two professors, two supervisors, and a private practice associate trained by renowned psychologist Carl Rogers at the University of Chicago. Such venerable mentors made invaluable contributions to my own personal and clinical growth. While a master's student at George Williams College, I was first exposed to one of Rogers's central concepts of client-centered therapy: empathy.

In his book, *Client-Centered Therapy*, Rogers wrote:

This formulation would state that it is the counselor's function to assume, in so far as he is able, the internal frame of reference of the client, to perceive the world as the client sees it, to perceive the client himself as he is seen by himself, to lay aside all perceptions from the external frame of reference while doing so, and to communicate something of this empathic understanding to the client.[29]

Alexy Shukin, our counseling department chair, took his doctoral studies with Rogers to heart. For two years, our core therapy courses focused on empathy. His heuristic approach was experiential. We continually gained knowledge and experience in classes, labs, and practicums and from supervision and student-teaching. At the time, I had no idea how valuable my training would be. The two-year master's program proved transformative and served as a singular influence on my development as a clinician. Just as importantly, I became a more sensitive human being. I intuitively sought to learn how others felt and to see the world from their perspective.

During my five decades of practice, I sat with thousands of individuals. Whether I met with a preschooler, child, adolescent, or adult, my goal was always the same: to let my patients know that I felt their pain, understood their feelings, and was genuine in my compassion. It was often a struggle for me to connect with my patients, given the severity of their problems. I treated many children who were socially withdrawn, highly nonverbal, or autistic. Given the nature of their presenting symptoms, social interaction and communication proved difficult. There existed a lack of social-emotional reciprocity. For children, I frequently provided play therapy, which was less threatening and gave them a chance to be themselves. We could still "engage" in proximity on the floor or seated across from each other while playing with toys or puppets or playing chess or other games. It was safer, less threatening, and imposed no pressure to carry on a conversation. Empathy is a valuable human resource even when the other person doesn't speak.

I recall treating an eight-year-old boy diagnosed with autism. For each of his weekly appointments, we sat on the carpet and played. Rather, he largely engaged in self-play, cut off, seemingly oblivious to my physical presence. Our sessions lacked social-emotional engagement, verbal communication, or any type of meaningful, noticeable interaction. After nine months, we enjoyed a major breakthrough. My patient entered, sat down, and began to speak to me in complete sentences. He had a smile on his face and was emotive. It was as if the prior nine months of non-verbalization had never occurred.

I gained tremendous insight from the case. I realized that people, especially children, have a built-in readiness. A child's self-trust and trust of others differs greatly. A central axiom of psychology is that all behavior is purposeful. We can never immediately or easily understand another person's external behavior. Conversely, the same can be said of our own inability to comprehend our behavioral responses—or lack thereof. Yet within close physical interpersonal space, we can develop a sense of trust, rapport, and even a therapeutic bond with few spoken words.

I also learned that being empathic and displaying genuine compassion for another human being is a powerful means of helping a scared or troubled child. Freud called psychoanalysis "talking therapy." Listening therapy, though, also matters. Both can be therapeutic. The key is to intuit which one is appropriate in the moment.

Throughout my training and development as a clinician, professors and supervisors stressed to me the importance of knowing my own tendencies. It's critical to not impose or project our own "stuff' onto the life of another person. Everyone deserves an independent, objective evaluation, an unbiased encounter, opinion, or assessment, "insofar as he or she is able."

I remember Dr. Alan K. Rosenwald discussing the most important asset of a child psychologist during class. "What's the main feature you must have to successfully treat children?" he asked.

No one had the right answer.

"Patience," he told us.

Treating the autistic boy reassured me that I possess patience and that therapy is a parallel, intersubjective journey for patient and therapist. Being acutely aware of and responding to nonverbal cues is just as valuable as acknowledging verbal communication. In both situations, providing a safe, trusting, accepting, and empathic milieu is what matters.

Empathy training is now a main component of many current programs to help children and adults change and grow. These efforts are taking place across the lifespan as both prevention and intervention in a multitude of settings, including daycare centers, schools, hospitals, and judicial systems.

CHAPTER 3: EMPATHY

The current emphasis on empathy training can be traced to one salient reason: it works. Individuals can be taught to be more caring and to perceive others from their own frame of reference. As clinical and scientific research studies show, empathy enhances prosocial behavior and the quality of relationships. Some recent findings are based on neuroscience research that measures neural reactivity and alterations in brain functioning.

For his dissertation research, one doctoral student studied the differential therapeutic effects of several different types of psychotherapeutic approaches. A single patient visited several different therapists. The researcher concluded that the patient found that most approaches helped her so long as she felt the therapists were empathic.

Formidable pioneers in child psychiatry and psychology, such as Freud and Jean Piaget, didn't believe that young children were capable of being empathic. Each postulated that children, by nature, are too egocentric. Their theory has been discredited by newer research. Data from the early 1970s onward reveals the highly sensitive, empathic capabilities of young children.

As a student at Oberlin College, I volunteered at an orphanage and visited Pablo, my assigned child, each Sunday. We went trick-or-treating on Halloween and afterward returned to the orphanage. The children, including Pablo, who usually collected the most treats, emptied their bags onto a long table in the dining room and shared their goodies with those children who hadn't gotten many treats or hadn't gone trick-or-treating. The children had committed a spontaneous, voluntary, and loving act of empathy and compassion.

Compassion and empathy have been a focus of discussion and research within many fields of psychology, including social psychology, developmental psychology, psychopathology, and neuropsychology. Until recently, however, precious little research has been conducted on the role of parent-child attachment as the underlying basis for a child's development of empathy. Two longitudinal studies ranging from fourteen to eighty months assessed the link between maternal-child attachment and empathy in community families. The findings indicate that security with mothers resulted in higher empathy. Insecure and non-empathic children, meanwhile, exhibited especially low prosocial behavior.[30]

Following empirical research on the association of maternal attachment and empathy, researchers studied the critical role of parental empathy in the development of the parent-child relationship. The findings indicate that parental empathy is positively related to children's security attachments, emotional openness, and perceptions of parental warmth.[31]

An underlying evolutionary and biological component is inherent in the concept of maternal empathy and childhood security. It presupposes that parents innately and automatically respond to the biological needs of their offspring. They behave in a compassionate and caring manner to protect their child's survival. "In 150 years," Charles Darwin stated, "humans will be more sympathetic." Bowlby[32] and Mary Ainsworth[33] related the critical role of empathy to evolutionary theory and emphasized maternal awareness and sensitivity to children's emotional cues as factors that motivate and shape consistent and contingent responsiveness.

CHAPTER 3: EMPATHY

The results of assessing parental empathy represent a new approach and model with which to study attachment and the development of prosocial behavior. Such an approach provides an opportunity to integrate the disciplines of clinical psychology, social psychology, cognitive science, developmental psychology, and neuroscience to better understand the core components and dynamics inherent in parent-child relationships. The newer models help predict early risk factors within families and have led to evidence-based intervention programs to teach and impart empathy.[34]

Psychologists generally agree that prosocial behavior and empathy are central to a child's emotional health. The capacity to care for others is a requisite component of a fully functioning, socially competent, happy, and thriving human being. Currently, many school districts are incorporating psychosocial and emotional learning into their daily classroom curriculums. The goal is to intervene and foster the development of empathy and positive social interaction in children at all age levels.

Social learning in the classroom allows children to become more adaptive and responsible. It also increases their capacity to self-regulate their impulses while becoming more "other centered" rather than egocentric. We can see another long-term benefit of social and emotional self-learning in the classroom: it lowers the risk of later onset of behavioral, antisocial, and personality disorders. Empathetic children are significantly less likely to externalize their anger or engage in aberrant behavior.[35]

Currently, psychologists are focusing on the importance of integrative emotion regulation in the development of childhood prosocial behavior. A child's capacity to regulate their impulses is a key component in social adaptation and allows them to regulate their emotions and select which emotions to display. A recent study assessed 240 sixth- and seventh-grade Israeli students. The authors concluded that integrative emotion regulation predicts student prosocial behavior through the mediation of empathy toward classmates.

A body of psychological research evaluates the correlation between aggressive and antisocial behavior and low levels of empathy in children. According to the hypothesis, the presence of high levels of affective empathy serves to prevent externalizing and aggressive behaviors. Researchers conducted an extensive review of the literature to measure the variables of low empathy and externalizing behaviors. Their findings noted substantial evidence of a modest negative relationship between empathy and aggressive behavior.[36]

Jean Decety

Jean Decety, the Irving B. Harris Distinguished Service Professor, is the director of the Child Neurosuite and head of the Social Cognitive Neuroscience Laboratory at the University of Chicago. Affective neuroscience, developmental social neuroscience, and developmental psychology lie at the heart of Dr. Decety's diverse research interests and skills, and those specialties have informed his intensive, prominent research and publications regarding empathy. Decety has edited eight books. Three of his books, in addition to several articles, focus on the neuroscientific underpinnings of empathy. He's arguably the leading neuroscientist conducting research on empathy.

Empathy

Empathy is a lived, shared emotional experience occurring within an intersubjective relationship. It can be defined as someone's capacity to emotionally perceive and experience the pain of another person. And it's essential for a person to develop in a socially and emotionally healthy manner because it underlies the capacity to engage in social perception and positive, mutually engaging social interaction. Scientific evidence and professional consensus confirm that empathy is highly associated with prosocial behavior, morality, and the regulation of aggression.

Our focus concerns emotional empathy, also known as affective empathy, which is defined as the ability to share the feelings of another person. Decety's critical examination of the underpinnings of empathy was conducted within the purview of both developmental and affective neuroscience. He identifies three distinct components of human empathy: (1) affective arousal, (2) emotion understanding, and (3) emotion regulation. Each component has a different developmental trajectory. In his article "The Neurodevelopment of Empathy in Humans," Decety writes:

> *These components are implemented by a complex network of distributed, often recursively connected, interacting neural regions, including the superior temporal sulcus, insula, medial and orbitofrontal cortices, amygdala, and anterior cingulate cortex, as well as autonomic and neuroendocrine processes implicated in social behaviors and emotional states. Decomposing the construct of empathy into subcomponents that operate in the*

healthy brain and examining their developmental trajectory provides added value to our current approaches to understanding human development. It can also benefit our understanding of both typical and atypical development.[37]

Social psychologist Dr. Nancy Eisenberg offers another definition of empathy:

In developmental psychology, empathy is generally defined as an affective response stemming from the understanding of another's emotional state or condition similar to what the other person is feeling or would be expected to feel in a given situation.[38]

Decety writes:

Recent affective neuroscience research with children and adult participants indicates that the affective, cognitive, and regulatory aspects of empathy involve interacting, yet partially overlapping, neural circuits. Furthermore, there is now evidence for age-related changes in these neural circuits which, together with behavioral measures, reflect how brain maturation influences reactions to the distress of others.[39]

Affective Arousal

As is the case in the early development of the infant's intersubjective self, the affective feature associated with empathy develops prior to the onset of cognition and reasoning. At birth, the infant already demonstrates affective arousal, which occurs between the mother and her neonate through bilateral,

CHAPTER 3: EMPATHY

intersubjective, sensitive, maternal responsivity. Child psychologist and psychobiologist Colwyn Trevarthen's research (more on this in chapter 9) explores the infant's motivation to evoke emotional responses from their mother's face and to respond to her touch and voice. Serve and return occurs within the context of maternal attunement to the baby's cues, smiles, and eye movements.

Infants emotionally respond and communicate primarily through their ability to perceive and respond to the faces of others. At birth, the newborn's drive for survival is primary, which means that he or she quickly becomes acutely aware of those other humans who are familiar and unfamiliar. The neonate innately perceives and emotionally acquires information regarding the feelings and intentions of others. For example, he or she knows "whether the caregiver is pleased or displeased, afraid or angry." Decety notes that affective responsiveness is known to be present at an early age, is involuntary, and relies on mimicry and somatosensory-motor resonance:

Discrete facial expressions of emotions have been identified in newborns, including joy, interest, disgust, and distress, suggesting that subcomponents of emotional experience and expression are present at birth, and supporting the possibility that these processes are hard-wired in the brain. Human newborns by ten weeks of age are capable of imitating expression of fear, sadness, and surprise, preparing the individual for later empathic connections through affective interaction with others.

    Together, these findings indicate that, very early on, infants are able to perceive and respond to another's affective state.

This automatic emotional resonance between other and self relies on a tight coupling between perceptual processing and emotion-related neural circuits. Infant arousal in response to the affects signaled by others can serve as an instrument for social learning, reinforcing the significance of the social exchange, which then becomes associated with the infant's own emotional experience. Consequently, infants come to experience emotions as shared states and learn to differentiate their own states partly by witnessing the resonant responses that they elicit in others.[40]

Emotion Understanding

Analogous to the precognitive intersubjective self in infancy involving mutual, shared emotional meanings, affective arousal can be explained within an emotional, proto-conversational stage of development. Emotion understanding, a component of empathy, also includes the cognitive domain and amounts to a more mature level of empathic awareness. Decety notes, "Such an understanding requires the formation of an explicit representation of the feelings of another person as an intentional agent, which necessitates additional computational mechanisms beyond the affect sharing level."[41] The cognitive components give way to empathic understanding over time, even though many precursors are already in place very early in life.

Dr. Paul L. Harris defines emotion understanding as follows:

Emotion understanding may be defined as the child's understanding of the nature, causes, and control/regulation of emotion, or as the way in which the child identifies, predicts, and explains emotion in him/herself and others.[42]

CHAPTER 3: EMPATHY

According to Decety, an emotional experience, as a state of mind, consists of affective *and* conceptual content. "Emotion is also, however, an interpersonal communication system that elicits response from others," he notes. "Thus, emotions can be viewed both as intrapersonal and interpersonal states, and the construct of empathy entails both such dimensions."[43]

Neuroscience employs two important strategies to help understand the flow of information processing and the ordering of knowledge. The first strategy is bottom-up. Sensory input is generally considered bottom-up; it lacks a higher level of direction and complexity in sensory processing. The second strategy is top-down. Higher cognitive processes are considered top-down because other sources provide more information.[44]

The above strategies help clarify Decety's take on emotion understanding:

Regarding the causes and effects of emotion and the cues used in inferring emotion, developmental research has detailed progression from stimulus-bound, behavioral explanations of emotion to broader, more mentalistic understandings. Children develop their emotional inferences, which contain a more complex and differentiated use of several types of information, such as relational and contextual factors in the goals or beliefs of the target child. This development appears to be somewhat slower for complex social emotions like pride, shame, or embarrassment.[45]

In explaining how humans develop an understanding of others' thoughts and feelings, Decety writes:

Regarding cognitive empathy, an individual employs perspective-taking processes to imagine or project into the place of the other in order to understand what she/he is feeling. These cognitive aspects of empathy are closely related to processes involved in Theory of Mind (ToM), executive function, and self-regulation. Growing evidence documents that executive function and ToM are fundamentally linked in development and that their relationship is stable... Emotion recognition and understanding continue to become more accurate well into adolescence.[46]

Theory of Mind

Decety provides new neuroscientific evidence, based on a top-down model, to understand the processing of information. He presents findings to support that "ToM is layered atop affective processes in its development and depends on the forging of connections between brain circuits for domain-general cognition and circuits specialized in social understanding. Neural imaging studies have identified a circumscribed neural network that reliably reinforces the understanding of mental states (of self and others) and links the medial prefrontal cortex (mPFC) with the posterior superior temporal sulcus at the temporoparietal junction (TPJ)."

"In sum," Decety writes, "the neural circuits implicated in emotion understanding partly overlap with those involved in ToM processing, especially the mPFC and right TP, and they still undergo maturation until late adolescence."[47]

CHAPTER 4

Play

> *"Play is the highest expression of human development in childhood for it alone is the free expression of what is in a child's soul."*
>
> — FRIEDRICH FRÖBEL

WHEN I SPEAK with friends or family about growing up, we usually talk about my most cherished childhood memory: playing. I have fond recollections of playing alone with toy soldiers, knights in a castle, or my Jerry Mahoney ventriloquist puppet—or performing magic tricks, or making forts or tunnels through the snow. When I wasn't playing alone, I engaged in "free play" with my friends. A buddy would drop by, or I'd go to his house, and we'd conjure up something to do. Sometimes we might stay inside and play with our trains or games. But usually, if the weather was good, we went outside to ride our bikes or play in the neighborhood park.

When I rode my bike through Prairie Park in East Chicago, Indiana, the towering cattails hid the inner areas and secret trails.

After I found a trail that took me to the hobo camp near the railroad tracks, I made a habit of visiting and talking with them before and after they jumped the passing trains. I would sit with them by the campfire and pass the time.

Pickup games of baseball, basketball, or football after school gave us the chance to play, exercise, and make new pals. In autumn, we would carry a push broom to the park to sweep off the leaves covering the tennis court so we could play tennis. If we were lazy, we might just hit the street and toss a football around. Before beginning, though, we might rake the leaves into a big pile and make a fire in the street gutter, throw on some baking potatoes, and eat them at "halftime." The alleys in my neighborhood provided another place to play. When we were little, we played hide-and-go-seek behind garbage cans. As we got older, we played basketball. My parents put up a backboard and hoop atop our garage. Those were happy times.

Fortunately, my parents didn't impose a curfew on me. They knew that I'd be hungry after running around so much and would be home for dinner or before it got dark. In our neighborhood, neighbors looked out for each other, which gave me a sense of freedom to roam, play, think, explore, grow, and just be a kid.

Today, most children don't have the chance to "free play." In many cases, children's daily routines lack playtime of any kind. Now, play is based on structured and programmed activities, and as soon as their children are old enough to participate, parents fill their calendars with play dates and structured activities like gymnastics, swimming, soccer, and dance. Such activities, in and of themselves, are rewarding. But children have little time to just play, unrestricted, without rushing here and there to a formal program or lesson.

Jaak Panksepp, the father of affective neuroscience, wrote:

When children are asked what they like to do more than anything else, the most common answer is "to play!" It brings them great joy. And, often, roughhousing play is the most fun of all, even though most investigators recognize other types such as "object play" and "fantasy play." Although thousands of papers have been written on the topic, play is still considered a frivolous area of inquiry among most neuroscientists. Only recently have some researchers become interested in the underlying brain issues. Now, increasing numbers of investigators are beginning to realize that an understanding of play may reveal some major secrets of the brain and yield important insights into certain childhood psychiatric problems such as autism and attention deficit disorders (or hyperkinesis, as it used to be known). It is now certain that the brain does contain distinct neural systems devoted to the generation of roughhousing or rough-and-tumble (RAT) play. Indeed, one of the best species for systematic study of this behavior is the laboratory rat and practically all the work summarized here is based on such play in rats. Although our knowledge about the underlying PLAY systems remains rudimentary, RAT play appears to be intimately linked to somatosensory information processing within the midbrain, thalamus, and cortex. Certain synaptic chemistries are especially effective in arousing play (e.g., acetylcholine, glutamate, and opioids) while others reduce playful impulses (e.g., serotonin, norepinephrine and GABA), but neuropharmacological studies tell us little about the adaptive function(s) of play. There is an abundant theoretical literature regarding these functions comparable to that found in dream research, but relevant data are decidedly scarce.[48]

The following description from a leaflet in a box of Lego® toys encapsulates the issue:

When children play, they exercise their senses, their intellect, their emotions, and their imagination—keenly and energetically. To play is to explore, to discover, and to experiment. Playing helps children develop ideas and gain experience. It gives them a wealth of knowledge and information about the world in which they live—and about themselves. So to play is also to learn. Play is fun for children. But it is much more than that; it's good for them, and it's necessary. Play gives children the opportunity to develop and use the many talents they were born with.[49]

Continuing his central theme of rough-and-tumble play, Panksepp writes:

Roughhousing PLAY systems appear to be conserved in the brains of many mammalian species, and we should be able to obtain a credible answer to the functional questions, even for humans, by carefully analyzing animal models. We anticipate that play will be found to have many beneficial effects for both brain and body, including the facilitation of certain kinds of learning and various physical skills. Most important, play may allow young animals to be effectively assimilated into the structures of their society. This requires knowing who they can bully and who can bully them.

CHAPTER 4: PLAY

One must also identify individuals with whom one can develop cooperative relationships and those whom one should avoid. Play probably allows animals to develop effective courting skills and parenting skills, as well as increasing their effectiveness in various aspects of aggression, including knowledge about how to accept defeat gracefully. It seems that most of the basic emotional systems may be recruited at one time or another during the course of play, and in higher organisms, play may encourage organisms to test the perimeters of their knowledge. In short, the brain's PLAY networks may help stitch individuals into the social fabric that is the staging ground for their lives. Is it any wonder, then, that play is such fun—perhaps one of the major brain sources of joy?[50]

Far too many children lack a sense of play nowadays. Such children are easy to identify. Typically, they present as sad and lethargic, and they lack energy and spontaneity. They seldom smile. Rather than engage in socially interactive, playful activities, they prefer to self-isolate and watch television, tablets, or computers. Play is an essential psychological resource or personality component inherent in healthy child development. Jaak Panksepp writes, "A great deal of joy arises from the arousal of play circuits within the brain. That play is a primary emotional function of the mammalian brain was not recognized until recently, but now the existence of such brain systems is a certainty."[51]

I found utilizing play therapy with my patients natural and fulfilling. Better still, relating to children at their level proved therapeutic. I largely employed play therapy with withdrawn or autistic children. This often meant sitting on the floor, finding their comfort zone, and going at their pace. My goal was to tap into their frame of reference—just as I would with anybody. When playing with frightened, emotionally guarded, socially detached children, I waited patiently. I learned to be highly sensitive to their nonverbal cues and to read their subtle, nuanced behaviors. So much of our behavior is nonverbal. Young children, especially those maintaining a protective shell around themselves, use nonverbal behavior as their primary language. Their verbal skills and capacity to be emotive don't evolve until they feel safe, which makes sense. Why would or should they trust a total stranger?

I rarely began play therapy—or any therapeutic intervention—with a firm, preconceived hypothesis regarding root causes. My therapeutic acumen didn't lie in plugging children's behavior into established theoretical, structured schemas. Instead, I relied on my ability to be patient, to listen carefully to each child, and to gauge the meaning of their behavior. In so doing, I helped develop a safe, trusting relationship and environment. Beyond that, we began a mutual blind journey of careful risk and trust. Of course, even without verbal communication, a genuine intersubjective relationship can develop. It requires the same conditions as any other intersubjective relationship—a face-to-face physical and emotional presence, empathy, and respect—and an emotional bond and dialogue are created when we meet them. The same type of personal attunement and responsiveness transpire within a responsive, sensitive parenting relationship. If these features are present, the child will feel safety, love, and trust. Then, and only then,

CHAPTER 4: PLAY

will the words and social-emotional interactions follow.

As mentioned in chapter 3, I treated an eight-year-old boy who had been referred to me with a diagnosis of autism. For seven months, we sat together on the carpet and slowly developed a relationship. He used our time to self-play, and we rarely interacted. Then, finally, without any warning or prior signals, he began to speak to me. To this day, this remains a precious moment for me. It speaks to the joy that comes from just being there for someone and showing patience and caring along the way. It also illustrates the concept of readiness in children. We all have our own timeline when it comes to risking, self-disclosing, and showing vulnerability and trust, particularly while in the company of a total stranger.

Friedrich Fröbel is considered the preeminent pioneer and proponent of play as an essential component of child education. His firm belief in "self-activity" led to his development in 1840 of the first formal early childhood educational program: kindergarten. Fröbel asserted that the teacher's primary purpose was not to drill children but to facilitate their self-expression and growth through individual and group play. He developed circles, spheres, and many toys, which he called "gifts" or "occupations." Their purpose was to foster learning through playful activities, often combined with songs and music. Additionally, Fröbel concluded that the most significant brain development occurs between birth and age three. He stressed the need to begin education earlier than had been previously thought necessary.[52]

Several scientific studies highlight the critical role of play in development and provide empirical data to support Fröbel's assertions. They emphasize the necessity of play in infancy and childhood to mediate healthy social, emotional, and cognitive development. The groundbreaking research of clinical psychologist Jerome Singer and his associates at Yale changed our understanding of imaginative play's role in development. Singer conceptualized a cognitive-affective approach that underscores how much human energy and activity is devoted to information processing. The two primary sources of information are internal sources and cues from the external world. Singer emphasizes the importance of the former because internal sources provide psychological value to children in terms of attention, concentration, frustration tolerance, and positive affect.[53] As Dr. Diana Shmukler, a professor and clinical psychologist, wrote in 1979:

The child's imaginative play can be seen as the genesis of internal processes of daydreaming and fantasy. In assimilating his experiences of the world, the child comes to grips with them cognitively and emotionally and expresses them in play.[54]

Such a formulation differs significantly from psychoanalytic theory, which focuses on the cathartic nature of play without the child having to deal cognitively with his external environment. Singer's emphasis on the child's inner world involves exploring the external environment and his own inner world. Such curiosity and exploration are then expressed in play. Shmukler explains the concept further:

(Singer) defines imaginative play as a controlled examination of novelty and gradual assimilation of that novelty, which is

accompanied by alternating positive effects of interest, surprise, and joy. The exploration is not of the physical environment but of the child's insufficiently assimilated experiences and fantasies, or memories, of adult interactions and communications.[55]

A direct association exists between a child's capacity to play imaginatively and their level of psychological wellbeing. American psychiatrist and author Roger Gould notes that "a child's inability to internalize a sense of imaginative play is symptomatic of pathology. In large measure, this is because one of the benefits of engaging in imaginative play in normal development is the opportunity to work through emotional problems. Without such an opportunity, abnormal development is highly probable."[56]

The empirical studies on imaginative play indicate that imaginative make-believe behavior is necessary for a child's socialization and cognitive development. As Singer wrote, "Imaginative play may be one of the great untapped resources in the amelioration of pathology in the developing socially constructive orientations in all children."[57]

While a fellow in clinical psychology at the Bronx Municipal Hospital Center of the Albert Einstein College of Medicine, Jan Drucker, PhD, studied the concept of play by observing how a two-year-old toddler handled developmental tasks. The study found that humans can deal effectively at a young age with complex developmental tasks presented simultaneously.[58]

In another experiment, Susan Crowley and Kathryn Sherrod studied seven-, ten-, and thirteen-month-old infants to assess parent-infant play during the first year of life. "The findings indicate the following: mother-infant play interactions change in quality during the latter half of the first year of life. Mothers shift from the predominant use of physical stimulation forms of play to a preference for games containing routinized roles that can be assumed by both partners. The data, more importantly, indicate that fathers follow a similar path of progress through developmental changes in play even though fathers and mothers differ in their use of rough play."[59]

Still another study, by Lauren Beaulieu and Jamie Povinelli, explored how to improve the solitary play of a typical preschooler. Researchers evaluated the effects of delivering specific instructions, such as "Complete these two puzzles while I read," and gradually increased the response requirements. The results showed that specific requirements improved the number of solitary play responses and the duration of engagement. During a treatment extension, a classroom teacher introduced a novel toy and observed an improvement in solitary play. The father, teacher, and preschool director found the treatment to be highly effective.[60]

The research of Jill Katz and Ester Buchholz indicates that the improvement in solitary play is an important finding for two primary reasons. First, it dispels the historically held belief that playing independently is harmful or ill advised because it does not involve social interaction. Now, to the contrary, psychological studies no longer contrast individual or solitary play versus social play. It is not that one is good and the other is disadvantageous. Rather, solitary play is a skill in and of itself. Second, increased solitary play is correlated with increased adaptive behaviors, such as problem-solving, appropriate responses to novel situations, and improved self-advocacy.[61] Moreover, increased solitary play is associated with a decrease in inappropriate behaviors. Keith Barnes's study shows that solitary play is developmentally appropriate for children between the ages of two and five years old.[62]

A qualitative ethnographic study by Helen Lynch and Alice Moore evaluated children's conceptualizations of happiness (as a proxy measure of wellbeing) amongst children living in Ireland aged six to eight years.[63] The research uniquely focused on the children's own perceptions and self-reports. Researchers collected data through visual, spatial, and language-based methods, and data analysis indicated three core themes based on the children's own points of view. The first theme indicates how the subjects perceived their overall sense of happiness (wellbeing), which basically involved play. The second theme describes the social and physical influences that shaped their participation in their valued play occupations. The third theme describes the social nature of relationships with people and animals.

According to one of the study's central findings, children's conceptualization of wellbeing consistently relates to play and playful occupation—with or without social partners. Additionally, the study indicates the complexity and degree to which children comprehend the influences on their happiness. Overall, this research, combined with other studies on play, reveals the pivotal and expanded role of play in a child's sense of happiness. Yet despite such empirical data, play is frequently overlooked or not assessed in the study of children's behavior. It should be considered a key, measurable variable within a framework of national standardized and normative scales.

Research shows an association between decreased playtime (during early education or due to rigid parenting) and poorer outcomes for children, but the long-term effects of playtime are less studied. In one study, Cliff McKinney and Leah Power assessed perceived parenting, playtime, and psychopathology as reported by 328 young adults between eighteen and twenty-five years old. The results demonstrated that perceived childhood playtime is associated with psychological adjustment in emerging adulthood.[64]

Most scientific studies of childhood play indicate that it is critical for cognitive and affective development and well-being. Yet many educational programs and institutions want to replace playtime with more formal, structured, academic learning models. Decreasing childhood playtime may negatively impact psychological adjustment.[65] Bruce Mallory and Rebecca New propose that an alternative solution is for schools to shift from individualistic models of learning and development to socialistic models of learning and development viewing the classroom as a community.[66]

Imagination, curiosity, and self-discovery are the magical realms through which children understand their world and develop. In a recent article, "The Power of Symbolic Play in Emotional Development Through the DIR Lens," Serena Wieder describes how symbols are formed and how emotional themes are symbolized. Children see themselves in the symbols they choose in play. She writes, "Children need play where interactive relationships with parents and caregivers help them climb the symbolic-emotional ladder, even when development is uneven, as in autism spectrum disorders."[67]

CHAPTER 4: PLAY

A secure initial parent-child attachment bond remains the basis and context within which such creative play occurs. The safe, trusting mother-child relationship and ensuing play interactions provide the opportunity for the child to explore, communicate, and understand the world. Dr. Serena Wieder, who is clinical director at the Profectum Foundation, asserts that symbolic play enhances "emotional development and embraces all developmental capacities."

The timetable for emotional and symbolic development differs for each child. Therefore, parents and caregivers must make room for multiple creative activities, including drama, art, music, dance, and reading. Children develop their abilities and appreciation for language, narrative, literacy, stories, history, art, and literature through symbolic play and symbolism. Symbolic play permits healthy psychological growth to occur as children begin to individuate and differentiate themselves from others. Each child learns that he or she is unique. Through experimenting with various roles and feelings, children gain the ability and opportunity to self-regulate their impulses and to function within societal norms. Such experiences of emotional self-exploration also foster a sense of empathy and prosocial behavior.

CHAPTER 5

Stimulation

"Tell me and I forget. Teach me and I may remember. Involve me and I learn."

— Xun Kuang

One day while working as a consultant to the school district, I met with a group of junior high school students—six in total, all boys. They had been referred to me for various behavioral problems they were exhibiting in the classroom, but all shared one primary feature: they were obsessed with gaming. I realized as much the second they entered my office.

"I got more kills last night than ever," one said as they sat down.

"It was so much fun playing with Tom and the new guy Larry," another said.

"I didn't go to sleep until one in the morning," a third added, "and really had a hard time getting up for school today."

A fourth nodded knowingly. "It's really cool. I've met so many new friends since I started playing Fortnite."

Fortnite, I was about to learn, is a survival video game that drops players onto a map and forces them to fend off "zombie-like creatures" while facing other challenges. It purportedly requires teamwork and world-building skills. My new patients would stay up quite late, even on school nights, to play the game and were so addicted to it they struggled to focus on therapeutic dialogue.

These young men were so deprived of the stimulus of healthy, inter-human interaction that all their focus was on gaming, which led to predictable behavioral and processing problems at school and also caused sleep deprivation, which had a further negative impact on their behavior and performance. They were, in fact, emotionally deprived.

In my work, I assessed and treated many children who were emotionally deprived. From infancy and throughout their childhood, such neglected children often lacked a primary caregiver. Having received minimal parental engagement, they were severely understimulated. Additionally, they seldom interacted with their peer group. They would typically return home from school to an empty house and were left to amuse themselves. Left to their own devices, they watched television, played games on the computer, or got into trouble. Many of my young patients would come home from school and just sleep.

Most children, even those not severely neglected, can experience a lack of stimulation to some degree. I can't count the number of children, many of whom were gifted, who told me over the years, "I'm bored." When conducting an initial interview, I would ask children and adolescents if they had a hobby or played a sport. The most common response was "No."

Some of those children said they were in a club or played an instrument. Understimulation refers to those times when a child's brain isn't receiving enough sensory input to keep them engaged with their surroundings.

Two primary forms of parent-child stimulation are emphasized in evidence-based scientific research: verbal communication and social interaction. In my clinical work, I noted another critical type of stimulation that was lacking: extracurricular activities. Its absence contributed to many children's boredom, malaise, and poor social skills.

Verbal Communication
Sandra Trehub notes that, in addition to touch, a mother's voice is special to an infant. Maternal communications, whether speech or singing, are vital in gaining an infant's attention, but infant-focused singing is found to be better than basic verbal communication for regulating infant emotion or arousal. The mother's voice appears to serve as a source of "security and stimulation" for infants. The stimulation simultaneously enhances both the maternal attachment bond and social, emotional, and cognitive growth.[68]

In an investigation of 6,377 mother-infant dyads, Melissa Page and her team studied the important role of maternal responsiveness and verbal stimulation in a child's social, emotional, and cognitive development. They found that maternal sensitivity and verbal stimulation predict increases in a child's social-emotional development. But only verbal stimulation contributes to cognitive development, especially when infants are older.[69]

Philip S. Dale et al. conducted a fascinating study in 2015 ("Why Does Parental Language Input Style Predict Child Language Development?"). The researchers represented several countries and interdisciplinary areas, and the collaboration included the Department of Speech and Hearing Sciences, University of New Mexico; the Department of Psychology, Tomsk State University, Russia; the Department of Psychology, University of York, United Kingdom; and the Social, Genetic and Developmental Psychiatry Research Center, King's College London, United Kingdom. The study had parents self-report their frequency of verbal interaction with their children consistently across cultures. The self-reports were independent of each situation and therefore accurately predicted early language acquisition.[70] The results of this study suggest that early parent-child verbal stimulation and bilateral interactions significantly increase the rate and quality of early language acquisition, regardless of the particular culture.

Social Interaction

Substantial evidence and opinion support the belief that emotions and regulation in children are the result of close relationships, especially with the mother and father. A child's emotional development occurs primarily within the mother-child dyad, according to research conducted by Tom Hollenstein et al.[71] Pamela M. Cole writes, "Emotions and emotion regulation occur throughout an individual's life, and such development is a socially regulated process."[72] Elsewhere, Eisenberg et al. state, "Researchers have considered the structure of emotion socialization, the patterns of bidirectional influences between mother and children, a keystone for many years."[73]

Extracurricular Activities

The continuation of childhood play evolves into participation in more organized activities. As children grow older, they enjoy increased opportunities to engage in an entire spectrum of activities, which provide avenues for continued self-integration, prosocial interaction, specialization, and enrichment. Such types of peer-based pursuit provide separation from parental presence and supervision. Likewise, they allow children time to develop social and emotional skills away from classroom learning assignments.

The shift away from family and school as the primary source of stimulation is critical to a child's development. Adolescents, in particular, require more than educational success to prepare for adulthood. Gaining increased social and emotional skills is as important to their development as acquiring cognitive skills. Neither parents nor teachers can give children the sense of self-confidence, emotional learning, new skills, pleasure, and friendships derived from extracurricular activities.

I've had the privilege of assessing or treating many children and adolescents. I saw many of those individuals in an acute-care inpatient hospital, residential treatment center, or juvenile detention center. Of the countless children I saw, I estimate that only about twenty adolescents were actively participating in an organized extracurricular activity. I often made the same recommendation in my psychological evaluations:

encourage the child to participate in some type of extracurricular activity.

In the cases involving juvenile delinquents, most of the teens had too much unsupervised leisure time on their hands after school. They weren't involved in school- or community-sponsored activities and lacked the camaraderie, positive peer group, adult role models, mentoring, discipline, team building, enjoyment, and expenditure of restless energy gained from organized sports, music programs, girls' and boys' clubs, dance lessons, science clubs, theater, chess, and other group-centered activities.

Children derive additional psychological benefits from organized activities that are structured, goal-oriented, collaborative, social, and focused on a common interest among participants. Such activities require behavioral constraints and the need for self-regulation, responsibility, and motivation, and they present an opportunity to find or develop an interest outside of school. As such, they moderate positive development outcomes in many areas, including self-esteem, identity, prosocial behavior, new skills, psychosocial adjustment, and social bonding. Research indicates that regular participation in such activities increases academic success and school attendance and decreases antisocial behavior. Organized activities play a crucial role in a child's ontogenesis. When built upon successive earlier successful stages of psychosocial development, organized activities positively influence an adolescent's ability to individuate.

In one 2003 study, entitled "Adolescents' Accounts of Growth Experiences in Youth Activities," Jodi B. Dworkin, Reed Larson, and David Hansen examined the developmental processes occurring during adolescents' participation in extracurricular and community-based activities. "Within ten focus groups, which totaled fifty-five adolescents, the subjects self-reported personal and interpersonal development. Their experiences consisted of experimentation and identity work, development of strategies for emotional regulation, and development of initiative skills, including setting goals and managing time. The interpersonal experiences measured included acquiring new peer relationships and knowledge, developing connections with adults, and developing group social skills, including assuming responsibility and team work. In almost all cases, the adolescents portrayed themselves as the agents of their own development and change. Regardless of the type of their recounted experience, the adolescents firmly felt that the change came largely from their own efforts. Sometimes they saw their development as individual, and sometimes they viewed it as collective or collaborative. But in all cases, they viewed it as their own doing. They listened, evaluated, and made the best decisions for themselves. This key finding underscores the influence of activities on solidifying and enhancing the adolescent's sense of responsibility, initiative, and individuality within intersubjective relationships."[74]

Based on the central finding in the study—that adolescents view themselves as being responsible—the authors suggest that adult leaders should shift their focus from teaching youth to helping youth teach themselves. Best-practice models of parenting and classroom learning mirror the findings of Drs. Jacquelynne Eccles and Jennifer Appleton of the Institute of

Medicine, National Academy of Sciences: "The most effective adults in adolescents' lives are not overly directive, but rather are responsive and provide structure, challenge, and support."[75] Such findings support the research of Milbrey W McLaughlin, who found that the best outcomes for youth programs occur when the programs are youth-centered and allow children to assume responsibility.[76]

In a 2003 study, Jennifer C. Anderson et al. established that for children to be positively involved in an extracurricular activity, parental support is critical. The authors examined children's perceptions of their parents' involvement in a wide range of activities. The purpose of the study was to advise parents on how to alter their level of involvement and minimize pressure to achieve a positive experience for their child. Two-hundred-and-thirty-eight elementary school students, ages nine to eleven, participated.

The results of the study suggest "that parental participation contributes to children's affective experience of participation in the activity in both positive and negative ways. Children viewed certain parental behaviors as positive and others as pressuring. The main finding makes clear that parents need to be sensitive to their child's interpretations of parental behavior. Additionally, parents need to understand and review their own motives that correlate their actions and responses to their child's performance. The takeaway? Parents must be aware of their ability to negatively impact their child's extracurricular activity. The parent's goal should be to behave in a non-pressuring manner that enhances their child's sense of enjoyment of the selected activity."[77]

Reading

The promotion of reading literacy falls under the aegis of the American Academy of Pediatrics. Reading is considered to be a necessary component of primary care pediatric practice. Because literacy directly stimulates brain development and social and emotional development, it's an essential topic of conversation with parents during office visits and carries the same weight as vaccinations, diet, exercise, and home environment. Reading proficiency by the third grade is the most significant predictor of high school graduation and career success, yet two-thirds of US third-graders lack basic reading skills.

The American Academy of Pediatrics issued a policy statement in 2014 pertaining to parents' involvement in their children's reading literacy. The salient findings and recommendations are as follows:

- Reading aloud regularly with young children stimulates optimal patterns of brain development and strengthens parent-child relationships at a critical time in child development, which, in turn, builds language, literacy, and social-emotional skills that last a lifetime.
- Research has revealed that parents listen and children learn as a result of literacy promotion by pediatricians, which provides a practical and evidence-based opportunity to support early brain development in primary care practice.
- Pediatricians should counsel parents about developmentally appropriate reading activities that are enjoyable for the child and the parents and offer language-rich exposure to books and pictures and the written word.

The AAP technical statements promote the "5 Rs" of early education:

1. Reading together as a daily fun family activity.
2. Rhyming, playing, talking, singing, and cuddling together throughout the day.
3. Routines and regular times for meals, play, and sleeping, which help children know what they can expect and what is expected from them.
4. Rewards for everyday successes, particularly for effort toward worthwhile goals such as helping, realizing that praise from those closest to a child is a very potent reward.
5. Relationships that are reciprocal, nurturing, purposeful, and enduring, which are the foundation of a healthy early brain and child development.

Children can and should be read to in infancy and the preschool years. It significantly increases their language skills and motivation to read. Additionally, this bilateral activity and time spent serves to enhance ongoing nurturing relationships.

Fairy Tales
"If you want your children to be intelligent," Albert Einstein purportedly said, "read them fairy tales. If you want them to be more intelligent, read them more fairy tales." Fairy tales can have a positive impact on a child's overall psychological development. Through folk tales and fairy tales, children receive vital messages, which typically involve some aspect of magic and good winning out against evil.

CHAPTER 5: STIMULATION

In the introduction to *The Random House Book of Fairy Tales*, Bruno Bettelheim explores the intrinsic value of fairy tales for children:

We do not know when or how fairy tales were invented. But as a form of literature handed down in the oral tradition, they are as ancient as any literature known to man. They were retold and listened to throughout the ages because they speak about man's fate, his trials and tribulations, his fears and hopes, and his most basic problems: in becoming and proving himself, in relating to his fellow men, and relating to the supernatural. The widespread preference of today's audiences for films such as Westerns and science fiction sagas such as Star Wars—all essentially fairy tales in modern disguise—shows that, as of old, these themes have much to offer to us today and to all ages, but particularly the young.

Freud recognized this when, in his paper on fairy tales, he wrote, "It is hardly surprising to learn through psychoanalysis what great importance fairy tales have for the psyche of our children." These tales are indeed of great help in the development of the psyche of the child. Children, on their own, are often unable to give name, form, or body to either their deepest fears or their most fervent hopes. Without fairy tales, these would remain formless and nameless, the shapeless anxieties which haunt every child as his nightmares, irrespective of whether he experiences them consciously and hence can recall them, or whether they remain repressed and obsess him therefore all the more. These nameless anxieties are much more intractable than well-defined ones, such as those which are described as being experienced by figures in fairy tales.

Taking in these stories permits the child to come to grips with his anxieties as he projects their causes onto evil figures he encounters in the stories, and as he gives body and with it concreteness to his fears in line with events told in the tales. Encountering his anxieties in story form permits the child to familiarize himself with them in an area once removed from his immediate experience, a most important first step toward objectifying and conquering them.

As readers become more familiar with a story and the solution it offers, they are also becoming able to devise methods to pacify their anxiety and thus protect themselves against what causes it.

Fairy tales assure the child that every evil phantom has its opposite which is more powerful in doing good than the evil figure is in doing evil, something the child may not be able to imagine all on his own when overcome by what, at the moment, seem to him the overwhelming difficulties of his life. It is the subtle balance between good and bad powers that is finally tipped in favor of the victory of virtue which gives the child the hope that in real life, his misfortunes will not only be limited in time, but will completely disappear, to be replaced by his elevation to a higher plane of existence where he will be secure for the rest of his life. While in reality there is not always a happy ending to our travails, it is the hope that there might be which sustains us, while without it we may fall into despair.[78]

Reading Tutoring Program

After receiving my master's degree, I worked at an elementary school as a school psychologist. The majority of students from grades K-6 within the district were several years behind in reading skills and comprehension as measured by standardized testing, so I decided to organize a voluntary districtwide program to tutor students after school. I worked with our local YMCA to obtain "Y Teens" as tutors. The school district and public library provided books for the children to read, a local church offered us space, and we acquired rugs upon which the student and tutor could sit—all in all, a comfortable, informal, and personable setting.

Each child was matched with a tutor, and their twice-a-week sessions lasted half an hour. Initially, the tutors read to the students. Later, the students were invited to read to them. The program lasted for one semester. When the program ended, I tested the children's reading comprehension and compared it to their prior standardized test scores. On average, each child's reading comprehension grade-level score increased by two years, with some improving even more. The results suggest that it's never too late to stimulate children to read and to facilitate the development of their reading skills. The program also demonstrated how an individualized, supportive, intersubjective relationship can enhance a child's self-esteem and motivation.

Tips to Help Your Child Enjoy Reading Aloud
The Committee on Early Childhood, American Academy of Pediatrics, offers the following tips:

- Read to your child every day, even if only for a few minutes. It's your time together.

- Reading should be fun. You don't have to finish a story if your child loses interest.
- Let your child choose the book, even if it means reading the same book over and over.
- Invite your child to "read" to you from a familiar book that he has memorized from having heard it read to him so often.
- Stop and ask about the illustrations or what your child thinks will happen next. The answers may amaze you.
- Read from a variety of children's books, including fairy tales, poetry, and nursery rhymes.
- Follow your child's interests in choosing the books. There are many great books on nonfiction subjects such as the ocean or dogs.
- Join your local library![79]

CHAPTER 6

Responsive, Sensitive Parenting

"To me, you will be unique in all the world. To you, I shall be unique in all the world."
— Antoine de Saint-Exupéry, *The Little Prince*

One day while working at my outpatient private practice in Homewood, Illinois, I received a call from a high school counselor. She asked if I could see—right away—a senior and his parents in her waiting room. She had just talked with the boy, Peter, who had told her he wanted to kill himself.

I saw the family that same afternoon. First, I spoke with Peter.

Peter was talkative. "My parents want me to be a doctor," he said as soon as he sat down. "That's all they talk about. They push me to take all AP [advanced placement] classes, especially in science. They're both doctors. They said they bought our house in this school district because it's highly rated. I told them I'm miserable because I don't like science and don't want to be a doctor."

"What are your interests?" I asked.

"I really like computers. Mostly computer animation and photography."

"That sounds really interesting." I studied Peter a moment. "Do you have a plan to harm yourself?"

"Yes, I do. I just can't take the pressure anymore."

I called Peter's parents in to join us and shared with them that their son was actively suicidal and should be referred to a psychiatric hospital for evaluation and treatment.

"That's not possible," the father replied.

"Why not?" I raised an eyebrow.

"Peter has final exams tomorrow."

Peter's father was so focused on his own selfish desires for his son's future that he downplayed the severity of Peter's mental state and refused to consider hospitalization. Even though he was a healthcare professional himself, he was insensitive to his son's welfare and insistent that Peter present for finals the next day at all costs, even though he had a suicide plan. When parents concentrate on their own desires and intentions, they can completely misread their children's cues and become blind to their needs and wellbeing.

We generally parent as we were parented. Parents who are physically absent or emotionally unavailable are merely re-creating the patterns and lack of maternal caregiving they experienced as children. The maternal attachment bond must be established at birth. There's no time to waste in forming this vital connection, which is essential to ensure a foundation for

CHAPTER 6: RESPONSIVE, SENSITIVE PARENTING

healthy emotional, social, and cognitive development.

The science of parenting indicates that development is a socially interactive process. A child's environment, both before and soon after birth, provides experiences that can modify genes and determine how and when they are expressed. Put another way, a child's life course and developmental stages aren't solely influenced by the effects of genetics. Environmental factors can mitigate and override the powerful influence of genes on a child's developmental course. An example of this environmental influence can be found in the development of executive function skills. Genetically speaking, healthy children are born with the ability to control impulses, focus attention, and retain information. The quality of caregiving and experiences during the first three years of life will provide the structure and foundation for the degree to which such skills will develop.

In his formulation of attachment theory, Bowlby defined responsive, sensitive parenting as follows: "Responsive, sensitive parenting refers to family interactions in which parents are aware of their child's emotional and physical needs and respond appropriately and consistently. Sensitive parents are 'in tune' with their children."[80]

Responsive, sensitive parenting is the best-practice model for a child's mother, father, and other significant caregivers. It provides the quintessential care necessary to satiate the infant's innate hunger for affect, nurturance, love, security, warmth, and safety. In fact, as will be discussed in chapter 11, affective neuroscience confirms that both infants' and mothers' brains are wired for such affective interrelatedness, responsiveness, and human-to-human bonding.

The Guide to Early Child Development (ECD), published by Harvard University, features a research-based section entitled "The Science of Early Child Development," and the "Working Paper by the National Scientific Council on the Developing Child."[81] Fifty years of intensive scientific research have been synthesized, translated, and operationalized into scientifically based best-practice models of effective parenting for healthy child development. We now can use cause-effect variables related to successful outcomes to predict successful early emotional, social, cognitive, and brain development.

The Guide to Early Child Development emphasizes three core concepts in early development, excerpted here:

1. *Experiences Build Brain Architecture*
   The basic architecture of the brain is constructed through a process that begins early in life and continues into adulthood. Simpler circuits come first, and more complex brain circuits build on them later. Genes provide the basic blueprint, but experiences influence how or whether genes are expressed. Together, they shape the quality of brain architecture and establish either a sturdy or a fragile foundation for all the learning, health, and behavior that follow. Plasticity, or the ability for the brain to reorganize and adapt, is greatest in the first years of life and decreases with age.
2. *Serve and Return Interaction Shapes Brain Circuitry*
   One of the most essential experiences in shaping the architecture of the developing brain is "serve and return" interaction between children and significant adults in their lives. Young children naturally reach out for interaction through babbling,

facial expressions, and gestures, and adults respond with the same kind of vocalizing and gesturing back at them. This back-and-forth process is fundamental to the wiring of the brain, especially in the earliest years.

3. ***Toxic Stress Derails Healthy Development***
   Learning how to cope with adversity is an important part of healthy development. While moderate, short-lived stress responses in the body can promote growth, toxic stress is the strong, unrelieved activation of the body's stress management system in the absence of protective adult support. Without caring adults to buffer children, the unrelenting stress caused by extreme poverty, neglect, abuse, or severe maternal depression can weaken the architecture of the developing brain, with long-term consequences for learning, behavior, and both physical and mental health.

How to Meet Your Children's Needs

The central feature associated with responsive, sensitive parenting is serve and return. Such interactions shape brain architecture. When an infant or young child babbles, gestures, or cries and an adult responds appropriately with eye contact, words, or a hug, neural connections are built and strengthened in the child's brain that support the development of communication and social skills. Much like a lively tennis match, this back-and-forth is both fun and capacity building. When caregivers are sensitive and responsive to a young child's signals and needs, they provide an environment rich in serve-and-return experiences.

Because responsive relationships are both expected and essential, their absence is a serious threat to a child's development and wellbeing. Healthy brain architecture depends on a sturdy foundation built with appropriate input from a child's senses and stable, responsive relationships with caring adults. If an adult's responses to a child are unreliable, inappropriate, or simply absent, the developing architecture of the brain may be disrupted, and subsequent physical, mental, and emotional health may be impaired. The persistent absence of serve-and-return interaction acts as a "double whammy" for healthy development: not only does the brain not receive the positive stimulation it needs, but the body's stress response is activated, flooding the developing brain with potentially harmful stress hormones.

Serve-and-return interactions make everyday moments fun and become second nature with practice. By taking small moments during the day to serve and return, we build up the foundation for children's lifelong learning, behavior, and health—and their skills for facing life's challenges. Child-adult relationships that are responsive and attentive—with lots of back-and-forth interactions—build a strong foundation in a child's brain for all future learning and development. Serve and return takes two to play!

Serve and Return: Five Steps for Brain-Building
The Center on the Developing Child (2017) walks us through the five steps involved in serve and return:[82]

1. *Notice the serve and share the child's focus of attention.*
   Is the child looking or pointing at something? Making a sound or facial expression? Moving those little arms and legs? That's

a serve. The key is to pay attention to what the child is focused on. You can't spend all your time doing this, so look for small opportunities throughout the day—like while you're getting them dressed or waiting in line at the store. Why? By noticing serves, you'll learn a lot about your children's abilities, interests, and needs. You'll encourage them to explore, and you'll strengthen the bond between you.

2. **Return the serve by supporting and encouraging.**

   You can offer children comfort with a hug and gentle words, help them, play with them, or acknowledge them. You can make a sound or facial expression—like saying, "I see!" or smiling and nodding to let a child know you're noticing the same thing. Or you can pick up an object a child is pointing to and bring it closer. Why? Supporting and encouraging rewards a child's interests and curiosity. Never getting a return can actually be stressful for a child. When you return a serve, children know that their thoughts and feelings are heard and understood.

3. **Give it a name!**

   When you return a serve by naming what a child is seeing, doing, or feeling, you make important language connections in their brain, even before the child can talk or understand your words. You can name anything—a person, a thing, an action, a feeling, or a combination. If a child points to their feet, you can also point to them and say, "Yes, those are your feet!" Why? When you name what children are focused on, you help them understand the world around them and know what to expect. Naming also gives children words to use and lets them know you care.

4. **Take turns... and wait. Keep the interaction going back and forth.**

   Every time you return a serve, give the child a chance to respond. Taking turns can be quick (from the child to you and back again) or go on for many turns. Waiting is crucial. Children need time to form their responses, especially when they're learning so many things at once. Waiting helps keep the turns going. Why? Taking turns helps children learn self-control and how to get along with others. By waiting, you give children time to develop their own ideas and build their confidence and independence. Waiting also helps you understand their needs.

5. **Practice endings and beginnings.**

   Children signal when they're done or ready to move on to a new activity. They might let go of a toy, pick up a new one, or turn to look at something else. Or they may walk away, start to fuss, or say, "All done!" When you share a child's focus, you'll notice when they're ready to end the activity and begin something new. Why? When you can find moments for children to take the lead, you support them in exploring their world—and make more serve-and-return interactions possible.

Keep these primary attributes of responsive, sensitive parenting in mind:

- It's a genuine I-Thou relationship.
- It's an ongoing interactive, collaborative, and sharing process.

CHAPTER 6: RESPONSIVE, SENSITIVE PARENTING

- It requires acceptance of your child as a unique person.
- It's a process of emotional interactions.
- It involves being intuitive and attuned to your child's immediate needs.
- It requires communication.
- It requires patience.
- It requires your physical and emotional availability.
- It requires your compassion and empathy.
- It requires unconditional positive regard of your child's unique mind.
- It requires imagination.

Responsive, sensitive parenting should be a birthright. Serve-and-return interactions, especially in infancy and the first three years of life, will shape brain development for life. The two ends of the spectrum of early child development—and consequent later-life adult functioning—are thrive and failure to thrive. These two levels of psychological health are the result of two very different parenting styles and environments.

I have assessed and treated thousands of severely neglected, abused, and deprived children, adolescents, and adults. I've seen and felt the effects of a lack of parental attachment and the consistent, ongoing, sensitive, and responsive attention, warmth, nurturance, and loving interactions necessary for healthy development. Such children are, in many cases, easily distinguished as different. Not unlike a malnourished, frail child, such children appear empty, lost, and emotionally hungry. They impress as sad and lonely. The lights in their eyes are dim, as are the flames in their souls—if they've been ignited at all. They lack the features and behaviors of a happy child: a bright-eyed countenance, a bounce in their step, laughter, enthusiasm, energy. The *joie de vivre*, spontaneity, is wholly absent. They're hungry for affection, emotional interaction with parents, attention, nurturance, and love.

These severely neglected children will never fully thrive. They suffer extreme psychic pain and experience a variety of learning problems, cognitive delays, social and behavioral difficulties, physical problems, mental health issues—even stunted brain development. The impact of toxic stress and the absence of responsive, sensitive parenting may result in permanent impairment. Despite the fact that neglect is by far the most frequent form of child abuse (see statistics in chapter 1), it is given less public attention than other types of abuse and receives a lower proportion of mental health services allocation.[83]

Mind-Mindedness

As a concept in developmental psychology, mind-mindedness refers to a caregiver's tendency to view their child as an individual with a mind, rather than merely an entity with needs that must be satisfied. Mind-mindedness involves adopting an intentional stance toward another person. Proposed by American philosopher Daniel C. Dennett, the intentional stance is a strategy for interpreting and predicting behavior that views organisms as rational beings acting in a reasonable manner according to their beliefs and desires (i.e. their intentions).[84]

Mind-mindedness differs greatly from parenting attitudes of past generations. The old-fashioned mantra, "Do what I say, not what I do," has been scientifically discredited and has been supplanted by a new responsive sensitivity to the uniqueness, idiosyncrasies, immediacies, and individuality of the wants and needs of our children. Serve and return, the ongoing caregiver-child interaction, is paramount because it promotes attachment and emotional growth—for child and parent alike. This ongoing social and physical interaction, both verbal and nonverbal, also facilitates normal psychosocial, emotional, cognitive, and brain development.

Researcher Elizabeth Meins is best known for coining the term and concept of mind-mindedness. This was her attempt to further operationalize and emphasize, in more depth, Mary Ainsworth's notion of sensitivity. In her paper, "Sensitive Attunement to Infants' Internal States: Operationalizing the Construct of Mind-Mindedness," Meins focuses on caregiving sensitivity and its association with mind-mindedness. The study also correlates the degree to which those two constructs predict infant attachment security.[85]

The Strange Situation

Mary Ainsworth, along with her colleagues, is best known for her classic research design of the "Strange Situation," a controlled procedure to assess individual differences in children's attachment behavior by observing an infant's reaction to stress. Here are the specifics of the paradigm:

The Strange Situation Procedure is divided into eight episodes, lasting for three minutes each. In the first episode, the infant and his or her caregiver enter into a pleasant laboratory setting with many toys. After one minute, a person unknown to the infant enters the room and slowly tries to make acquaintance. The caregiver leaves the child with the stranger for three minutes and then returns. The caregiver departs for a second time, leaving the child alone for three minutes. It is then the stranger who enters and offers to comfort the infant. Finally, the caregiver returns and is instructed to pick up the child. As the episodes increase the stress of the infant by increments, the observer can watch the infant's movement between behavioral systems: the interplay of exploration and attachment behavior, in the presence or absence of the parent.[86]

Dr. Ainsworth conducted her pioneering study at Baltimore while she was serving as an associate professor of developmental psychology at Johns Hopkins University. In the experiment, researchers placed twenty-six children into three different classification groups depending on their behaviors.[87] Each grouping represented a different classification of attachment or relationship with their caregiver. The results revealed that there are different types of communication, emotion regulation, and responses to perceived threats associated with each unique classification grouping. The three classifications of communication are as follows:

1. **Anxious-Avoidant Insecure Attachment**. This type of child avoids or ignores their caregiver and reveals little emotion, whether the caregiver leaves or returns.
2. **Secure Attachment**. This type of child explores freely in the presence of their caregiver and easily displays emotion.

3. **Anxious-Resistant Insecure Attachment.** This type of child reveals distress, even prior to separation, and is clingy and difficult to comfort when the caregiver returns.

Ainsworth's seminal research paradigm and findings have served as the basis for many of the subsequent empirically based, clinically significant outcome studies and currently accepted best-practice models of parenting. Meins's definition of mind-mindedness, found in "Sensitive Attunement . . .," is as follows:

Mind-mindedness is defined as caregivers' tendency to treat their young children as individuals with minds of their own, and enables caregivers to "tune in" to what their infants may be thinking or feeling. They focused on the core features of sensitivity—awareness and accurate interpretation of the infant's cues, and appropriate and prompt response to them—in developing the construct of mind-mindedness in the first year of life.[88]

Meins argues that researchers, practitioners, and especially caregivers must share Ainsworth's emphasis on the ability of the caregiver to understand the child's thoughts, feelings, and internal frame of reference. In conceptualizing maternal sensitivity, Ainsworth wrote that the sensitive mother is "capable of perceiving things from the child's point of view and respecting the child as a separate person."[89] The insensitive mother, meanwhile, attempts to "socialize with the baby when he is hungry, play with him when he is tired, and feed him when he is trying to initiate social interaction."[90] This accounts for the child's degree of attachment bond and consequent security.

Furthermore, a responsive, sensitive mother doesn't just respond to her child's cues; she accurately reads them and interprets her child's specific needs and wishes. The sensitive mother can respond so appropriately because her attunement is based on intimate interactions, keen observations, and trial and error as to what works in each specific situation. The mother can match the cue with a certain mental state in the child. The ongoing serve and return and subsequent feedback loop allow the mother to continually refine her responses to meet the ever-changing, nuanced needs of her child. She can gauge the effectiveness of her maternal response by accurately assessing whether it was well received and altered her child's mental state. In this regard, maternal sensitivity can only be assessed and understood within the mother-child dyad.

Again, according to Meins, when the caregiver engages and interacts in a highly attuned manner, a high level of secure attachment develops. If a caregiver is non-attuned—i.e., reveals little mind-mindedness—the child falls within the avoidant or resistant grouping. Meins's formulation of mind-mindedness augments Ainsworth's conceptualization of maternal sensitivity and allows for more specific observations and measurements of attunement and sensitivity.

The lack of highly attuned, sensitive, consistent serve-and-return interactions prevents the child from acquiring a secure attachment, which results in an increased need for the child to receive essential maternal care to satiate needs for affection, nurturance, and safety. Without a physical presence, perceived emotional warmth, and mutual intersubjective bond, delays in social, emotional, and cognitive development are likely. Indeed, maternal and paternal neglect and deprivation during the formative stages of development increase the risk for later onset of psychological disorders. The infant's innate need for affection, security, and emotionally intimate connection is critical.

Can mind-mindedness predict attachment security in the "strange situation" at twelve months? The findings indicated "that their designed index of mind-mindedness independently predicted infant-mother attachment security—the first empirical evidence that maternal attunement, specifically related to an infant's internal states, facilitates secure attachment."[91]

Ainsworth's paradigm continues to be the standard in the field of child development when studying attachment theory. Those who follow in her footsteps can explore in a laboratory setting the pioneering work of Bowlby to explain how early caregiving influences subsequent development. Moreover, such early studies permit researchers to identify the specific developmental paths associated with each of the three attachment patterns and other variables associated with each pattern.

While investigating the hypothesis that differences in socialization of affect accompany the three major attachment patterns, researchers reviewed videotapes of "strange situation" reunions for ten secure, ten avoidant, and ten resistant one-year-olds to examine maternal responses to infants' positive, neutral, and negative affects. The data suggest that each attachment pattern is associated with a unique pattern of socializing emotion.

Mothers of infants in the secure group attended to the full range of affective display and responded more frequently than those in other groups. They also made more comments about emotions and information. The authors conclude, "Secure infants, therefore, receive the message that all emotions are acceptable, and that emotions are a topic for discussion. Secure infants did, in fact, express the full range of emotions: a predictable outcome of the pattern of response shown by these mothers."[92] Secure-group mothers best satiated their children's affect hunger.

Mothers of avoidant infants were less responsive and were especially unresponsive to the little negative affect their infants expressed. They made the fewest comments about emotion and exceeded other mothers in distracting and comforting when their infants hadn't provided a clear affective case. The authors conclude, "They convey the message that emotions are not explicitly recognized, particularly negative emotions, and that it is the other, not the self, that sets the emotional agenda." As a group, avoidant infants were least expressive, and negative affect was rare in the observed reunions. Insecure infants showed a decrease in positive affect over the first two years of life, which is consistent with the avoidant pattern.[93]

Mothers of resistant infants were more responsive than those in the avoidant group, especially to negative affect, but responded minimally to positive affect. Ainsworth et al. conclude, "However, their comments about emotion were limited as in the avoidant group. The message to these infants was a mixed one. Negative affect will reliably get attention, but emotions are not to be discussed." The authors, observing a high level of fussing and crying among infants in this group, attributed it to the mixed messages being sent by their mothers. As explained in Ainsworth's original description of the infants' behavior within the resistant pattern, he or she presents with extreme passivity and helplessness—or tantrums and fussing—appearing to not know what he or she wants.[94]

Meins and a team of researchers investigated the correlation between maternal mind-mindedness and children's later understanding of mind. They obtained initial mind-mindedness measurements from infant-mother interactions at six months and from maternal interviews at forty-eight months of infant age, and they assessed children's understanding of mind by using theory of mind tasks at forty-five and forty-eight months and a stream-of-consciousness task at fifty-five months. Path analyses indicated direct correlations between mothers' use of appropriate mind-mindedness comments and children's later understanding of mind. Again, the conclusion is that mothers' affective responsiveness and explicit and appropriate talk regarding their infants' mental states is integral to facilitating children's developing understanding of mind.[95]

The new science of child development underscores the importance of the emotional domain in responsive, sensitive parenting in early child development and future optimal development. Responsive, sensitive parenting helps to form the child's initial sense of affectivity and serves as the foundation for forthcoming cognitive and brain development.

Researchers use two different theoretical frameworks to study responsive parenting. The first, the widely accepted primary principle of attachment, focuses on the caregiver's affective-emotional style.[96] The key attributes associated with positive parenting and secure attachment include warmth and nurturance, which are combined with the parent's capacity to read their child's cues and to accept and treat their child as a unique individual with their own mind and needs. The second, a sociocultural theoretical framework, adds the dimension of the cognitive domain.[97] Cognitively responsive behaviors, such as maintaining the child's focus of interest, are included, as is precise verbal input that is sensitive to the child's signals.[98]

In both frameworks, ongoing parent-child social interaction, or serve and return, allows the infant to develop a sense of attachment security and to feel safe to explore their world through verbalizing, physical movement, and thinking. A consistent parent-child dyad permits the child to develop a greater degree of insight into and attunement to their own cues and mind. Such responsive, sensitive parenting allows the child to internalize their own models and representations of appropriate emotionality and to individuate with a unique mind of their own.

Within the field of child development, the consensus is clear: responsive, sensitive parenting is the essential component for healthy growth and a secure maternal-child attachment. The unanswered question, however, concerns the timing and emphasis of responsive parenting. While scientific studies and literature reviews discuss the importance of responsive, sensitive parenting in early infancy, few studies have investigated the optimal timing for responsive, sensitive parenting during other stages of child development.

CHAPTER 6: RESPONSIVE, SENSITIVE PARENTING

In a classic study, "A Responsive Parenting Intervention: The Optimal Timing Across Early Childhood for Impacting Maternal Behaviors and Outcomes," Susan Landry and her team determined that optimal timing is dependent on two factors: the specific targeted behaviors and the degree to which the behaviors corresponded to a child's changing developmental needs. The authors conclude that a responsive parenting style must include behaviors from both attachment and sociocultural frameworks to be effective in influencing a child's development. An integrated conceptual model, including maternal-contingent responsiveness and warmth and the support of children's attention skills, served as the best explanation of positive effects on social and communication skills.[99]

Emotions are critical in parenting. Strong feelings like love, anger, joy, and fear are constantly experienced by a caring parent. The newborn's affect hunger is an innate craving that must be satiated with warmth, nurturance, and affection for initial survival and future healthy development. Touch is our first language and welcomes us into the world. It reassures us that we are alive and safe. The central nervous system expects positive emotions' vital signals, and emotional cues begin to wire the brain and lay the initial bottom-up affective foundation for future biological, psychological, cognitive, and social development.

The transference of such intrinsic, intuitive, and unconscious emotions also fulfills a mother's need to nurture, stimulate, and love her child. A mother's ability to engage in a responsive, sensitive interaction with her child, to begin to understand their unique mind and cues, forms the serve-and-return relationship, which will facilitate a sense of growth, safety, and trust for both child and mother. Through such a vital conduit and dyad, the infant will attach, satiate affect hunger, and eventually individuate and thrive.

Fifty years have passed since I first studied the Rorschach "T" or texture response. I've always been fascinated by the texture response as an index of a person's degree of affect hunger. When conducting psychological assessments, I inevitably found a high "T" score among children and adults who had poorly or never attached to their mother. Such individuals had typically received negative emotions and/or had been neglected or abused. In all cases, they had been deprived of initial and successive responsive, sensitive parenting. They felt an intense void or affect hunger. They intuitively craved what they had never received. In the extreme, some individuals had never received maternal affection during their formative years. Their mothers had been emotionally and/or physically unavailable. Such individuals can be diagnosed as "failure to thrive."

I realized early on in my career that children seek their mother's love and positive emotions, no matter how high the cost. They'll even seek negative attention if it means getting a response from their parents. Being emotionally neglected, children have told me, is more painful than being physically abused. Most children who elope from a residential treatment center run directly home. Their innate craving is to return to their birth mother to satiate their needs for warmth, nurturance, and safety. Such needs have been imprinted on our brain after millions of years of evolution as a social animal. Only our mother can fulfill what amounts to a survival instinct, which is to have our emptiness and longing soothed. A lack of maternal sensitivity in the formative years, meanwhile, has life-long consequences. Normal stress enables the brain and affective system to develop a sense of resiliency and ability to manage daily stress, but when a child is exposed to continual toxic stress, they lack the internal psychological mechanisms and normal brain development to be resilient.

The initial affective organization and bottom-up brain development forms the foundation upon which the brain will develop and later process higher-order cognition, executive functions, and social information. Healthy child development depends on recognition, understanding, and discussing of emotions. The APA Dictionary of Psychology notes the following:

Affective development pertains to the emergence of the emotional capacity to experience, recognize, and express a range of emotions and to adequately respond to emotional cues in others.

Bowlby, Ainsworth, and Meins provided working models of parental cues internalized by a child within the context of the attachment bond. The concept of mind-mindedness reminds us that a child utilizes and mimics their mother's emotional messages. In this way, a mother's emotions are transferred to the child via the warm, responsive, sensitive attachment bond.

Dr. Ted Dix's research examines parenting competence and its role in developmental risk in the first five to eight years of life. He has studied moment-to-moment processing factors that regulate parents' and children's emotional states, parents' ability to coordinate parent-child exchanges, and the tendency of the dyad to achieve mutual goals cooperatively:

> *Emotions are vital to effective parenting. When invested in the interests of children, emotions organize sensitive, responsive parenting . . . In harmonious relationships, emotions are, on average, positive because parents manage interactions so that children's and parents' concerns are promoted.*[100]

Mentalizing, in psychological terms, refers to a person's ability to interpret the underlying thoughts, emotions, and intentions behind someone's behavior (ours and others'). Meins and her colleagues examined the development of symbolic mentalizing abilities in thirty-three children whose attachment security had been assessed in infancy. The findings suggested the following: (1) securely attached children were better able to incorporate an experimenter's play suggestions into their sequences of symbolic play at thirty-one months; and (2) securely attached children performed better on a transfer task at age four. Additionally, the results suggested evidence of superior mentalizing abilities among the secure group at age five, despite no differences assessed in cognitive ability. The authors conclude that the security-related differences were likely due to the mothers' tendency to treat their securely attached children as individuals with minds.[101]

Research has also found that children who were raised in families where feelings were regularly discussed performed better on mentalizing tasks.[102] And researchers have noted two other security-related differences associated with the development of mentalizing: (1) mothers of securely attached children are more sensitive to their children's needs, and (2) mothers of securely attached children are more prone to invoke mental states in describing the behavior of others.[103]

Meins's longitudinal study provides scientific evidence to support the belief that certain features of the infant-mother caregiver relationship, especially the mother's responsive, sensitive tendency to interact with her infant as an individual with a mind, are highly associated with later development of symbolic and mentalizing abilities. Meins and her colleagues concluded as follows:

In the meantime, however, we can suggest that by treating their children as individuals with minds rather than creatures with needs which must be fulfilled, mothers of securely attached children can provide a creative social mirror, which allows their children to develop a sense of themselves as sources of perspectives on the world and thus to "think of themselves as (themselves) as thinkers."[104]

Maternal Attunement

The presence of maternal attunement is a key component of responsive, sensitive parenting and was first described by psychiatrist Daniel Stern, a pioneer who, for more than thirty years, worked in research and practice in infant developmental psychology. As well as passionately and meticulously observing infants and clinically reconstructing their early experiences, he focused on affective mother-child bonding. His research findings continue to influence the current best-practice models of development and parenting.

The APA Dictionary of Psychology defines attunement as follows:

The matching of affect between infant and parent or caregiver to create emotional synchrony. The parent's response can take the form of mirroring (e.g., returning an infant's smile) or be cross-modal (e.g., a vocal response "uh oh" to the infant's dropping cereal on the floor). Attunement communicates to the infant that the parent can understand and share the infant's feelings.

In his book, *The Interpersonal World of the Infant*, Daniel Stern describes selective attunement:

Selective attunement is one of the most potent ways that a parent can shape the development of a child's subjective and interpersonal life. It helps us account for "the infant becoming the child of his particular mother." Attunements are also one of the main vehicles for the influence of parents' fantasies about their infants. In essence, attunement permits the parents to convey to the infant what is shareable, that is, which subjective experiences are within and which are beyond the pale of mutual consideration and acceptance. Through the selective use of attunement, the parents' intersubjective responsivity acts as a template to shape and create corresponding intrapsychic experiences in the child. It is in this way that the parents' desires, fears, prohibitions, and fantasies contour the psychic experiences of the child.

CHAPTER 6: RESPONSIVE, SENSITIVE PARENTING

The communicative power of selective attunement reaches to almost all forms of experience. It determines which overt behaviors fall inside or outside the pale (Is it "all right"—within the intersubjective pale—to bang toys hard and noisy? To masturbate? To get really dirty?). It includes preferences for people (Is it all right to find delight in Aunt Ronnie but not in Aunt Lucy, who then says, "My nephew just doesn't take to me"? And it includes degrees or types of internal states (joy, sadness, delight) that can occur with another person. It is these internal states rather than overt activities per se that we will focus on most, since they have generally been less emphasized in this context.[105]

A study explored individual differences in mothers to determine if such representations of their own early childhood attachment relationships impeded or facilitated the recognition of their infant's experiences and needs. The findings indicated that securely attached mothers are more attuned to their babies than mothers who are insecurely attached. A key conclusion was that secure mothers attune to a range of infant affect, whereas dismissive mothers tended not to attune to negative affect.[106]

An axiom of psychology is that a child's perception of the world is directly affected and shaped by their parents' feelings about them and themselves. Yes, development research studies also look at variables like temperament, sex, birth order, and gender, but owing to the science of child development and the vital role of responsive, sensitive parenting, we now know that a child's emotional development is directly influenced by the affective tone and secure attachments of their earliest relationships. Positive affect and emotional warmth and acceptance allow the infant to develop self-esteem, meaning, trust, and self-regulation.

The emotional synchrony or matching of affect between infant and parent or caregiver assures the infant that his parents understand his needs and mind and that his own feelings are shared within a mutual, interactive relationship. He knows that he isn't alone in the world. He can depend on a loving, warm caregiver attuned to his emotions. Such vital responses and sensitivity to cues are experiential and emotional. The secure base derives from blind intuitive trust and primitive biological survival, but this secure attachment will evolve into cognitive representations and expectations of continued parental responsiveness and attunement. Bowlby referred to such expectations as "working models."[107] These models will continue to develop and be shaped, refined, and tested throughout childhood and adolescence and will become integrated into the adolescent's identity, serving as a core component of his own affective organization.

Larissa G. Duncan et al. find that mindful parenting involves a set of skills or practices that extends the concept of mindfulness to the context of parent-child relationships. It reflects the way parents integrate the concepts of mindfulness into their thoughts, feelings, and parenting behaviors, bringing an attitude of compassion, acceptance, and kindness to the parent-child relationship and being fully present during parent-child interactions.[108] The following key dimensions of mindful parenting are grounded in scientifically rigorous research conducted by Susan Bogels and Kathleen Restifo:

CHAPTER 6: RESPONSIVE, SENSITIVE PARENTING

1. Listening with full attention to the child
2. Non-judgmental acceptance of the self and child
3. Emotional awareness of the self and the child
4. Self-regulation in the parenting relationship
5. Compassion for the self as a parent and for the child[109]

Research correlates mindful parenting with several positive psychosocial outcomes in adolescence. Only a few such studies, though, have explored the mechanisms underlying that association. Helena Moreira and her team investigated whether the link between mindful parenting and adolescents' wellbeing is mediated by adolescents' attachment representations, self-compassion, and mindfulness skills. The study's sample comprised 563 parent-child dyads (95.6% mothers), with adolescents (61.5% girls) showing a mean age of 14.26 years. Parents completed a measure of mindful parenting, and adolescents completed measures of attachment representations, self-compassion, mindfulness, and wellbeing. The findings indicate that self-compassion and mindfulness appear to develop within a parent-child relationship marked by affection, self-regulation, and mindful awareness. Those two resources, combined with mindful parenting and positive representations of the parent-child relationship, are correlated with adolescents' wellbeing. The study revealed more:

Adolescents raised in secure and supportive family environments may internalize the soothing qualities of a responsive and compassionate attachment figure, such as a mindful parent, and develop a healthy self-to-self relationship characterized by compassion toward the self. They may also develop adaptive emotion regulation strategies and, consequently, develop a higher capacity for self-awareness.[110]

Researchers Claire Farrow and Jackie Blissett were among the first to study the role of maternal mind-mindedness and infant feeding interactions. In their research, the authors assessed the associations between maternal mind-mindedness at six months of infant age and later observed sensitivity and feeding behaviors with children at one year. Maternal mind-mindedness proved greater in mothers who had breast-fed compared to those who had formula fed. Controlling for breastfeeding, Farrow and Blissett observed a correlation between mind-mindedness and more sensitive and positive feeding behaviors at one year of age. The study also showed an association between mind-mindedness and greater general sensitivity in play, and this general parenting sensitivity mediated the effects of mind-mindedness on more sensitive and positive feeding behaviors. The authors noted the following:

> *The findings of this research indicate that, in addition to training about what and how to feed children, interventions should also focus on promoting caregiver attention to the child's autonomous thoughts, intentions, and feelings around mealtime. By elevating mind-mindedness, this could help to foster more sensitive and positive feeding behavior, which may ultimately benefit child health and wellbeing.*[111]

The science of child development establishes several key axioms, including the tenet that children who receive responsive, sensitive care from parents form more secure attachment relationships. Such children have a greater capacity to manage stress. Their secure attachment is critical in the child's development of resilience, which the APA Dictionary of Psychology defines as follows:

> ... *the process and outcome of successfully adapting to difficult or challenging life experiences, especially through mental, emotional, and behavioral flexibility and adjustment to external and internal demands.*

Self-compassion and compassion are essential features of responsive, sensitive parenting and caregiving. These attributes or personality features serve to support the development of children's resilience to stress. Additionally, they enhance the attachment bond by providing a soothing, secure, and safe relationship.

Until recently, psychologists focused on helping parents manage their children's behavioral problems. Experts emphasized observed symptoms, or "faulty" or "inappropriate" behaviors, and suggested interventions based on cognitive-behavioral models and behaviorist models. Such an approach has given way to a best-practice model based on the new science of child development. The parent-child relationship and the child-centered approach, based on sensitivity, attunement, and serve and return, foster healthy child development and emotional and cognitive growth and wellbeing. Barbara Burns and Yaffa Maritz write the following:

There is overwhelming evidence, from brain science to psychiatry, that young children who receive responsive and sensitive care from parents and caregivers have more secure attachment relationships and are better able to handle challenges and stressors in their lives.

Since ancient times, it has been recognized that parents influence their children's development. Across the last forty years, many structured parenting programs have been implemented that provide parents with skills and education to prevent, control, and manage problems in their children's behavior. In this same time period, researchers studying children's attachment have convincingly demonstrated that the parent-child relationship is the most significant and influential component in a child's life. Rather than focus on children's behavior problems, the groundbreaking studies done by David Winnicott, John Bowlby, Mary Ainsworth, Elizabeth Meins, and many others have shown that children thrive when they have a secure base from which to launch, right from the very beginning of their lives. This secure base is formed by having a loving primary caregiver who is sensitive, attuned to the child's internal world, and able to make sense of the child's nonverbal cues and respond affectionately and contingently in order to meet the child's needs. Attachment theorists have established that repeated and predictable experiences shape the way the child learns to see the world as a safe, reliable, and loving place.[112]

Donald Woods Winnicott, an English pediatrician, psychoanalyst, and pioneer in developmental psychology, is recognized for his ideas on the true self and false self, the "good enough" parent, and the transitional object. His seminal work on the good enough parent, in particular, has influenced the advancement of attachment theory and sensitive parenting. Between 1943 and 1966, Winnicott gave over sixty talks about child development on the BBC in the UK. His first talk was entitled "Happy Children." He believed that the first three years of a child's life formed a critical stage because a child develops an increasing sense of a genuine self in relation to larger groups of people.

As a pediatrician working with children and their mothers, Winnicott formulated his theoretical framework of the "holding environment" and noted that "the foundations of health are laid down by the ordinary mother in her ordinary loving care of her own baby."[113] The primary example of such care was the mother's attentive holding of her child. He expanded on this conceptualization by stating that "the mother's technique of holding, of bathing, of feeding, everything she did for the baby, added up to the child's first idea of the mother." He also asserted that, by experiencing a "good enough" mother, the infant develops the capacity to experience the body as the place in which one securely lives. Winnicott further extrapolated his concept of holding from mother to objects and relations in the outside world. He viewed healthy child development as "the continuation of reliable holding in terms of the ever-widening circle of family and school and social life."[114]

Burns and Maritz note:

Winnicott described caregiving as a complex and shifting dance of adaptation. He argued that through a caregiver's attunement with the child's inner world, environmental challenges can be calibrated to the child's developing abilities in order to best handle challenge, frustration, and stress. Minor misattunements, termed "minor impingements" by Winnicott, provided the child with opportunities to master stressful situations and strengthen frustration tolerance. Major misattunements resulted in overwhelming stress and frustration for the child resulting in maladaptive reactions and the creation of emotional defenses.[115]

Winnicott published five books and more than two hundred research articles. His writing and theoretical framework emphasized the important role of empathy and imagination in parenting. The philosopher Martha Nussbaum, an advocate of Winnicott's theories, noted that Winnicott underscores "the highly particular transactions that constitute love between two imperfect people."[116] Patrick Casement wrote, "Winnicott remains one of the few twentieth-century analysts who, in stature, breadth, minuteness of observations, and theoretical fertility, can legitimately be compared to Sigmund Freud."[117]

Distinguishing sensitive from insensitive caregiving and understanding how to reinforce the quality of compassionate caregiving are essential to the new science of parenting. Peter Fonagy and Charles Zeanah, having conducted many research studies investigating key factors associated with differences in caregiving, used two primary qualities to differentiate sensitive from insensitive caregiving: strength in adult reflectiveness and empathy for children. Higher levels of reflectiveness and empathy correlate with more sensitive caregiving.[118]

A recent theoretical proposal by Paul Gilbert has advanced the knowledge of sensitive caregiving. Gilbert's model emphasizes the vital role of compassion in the process of responsive, sensitive parenting. He notes that compassion is significant in soothing the infant and child and providing a sense of contentment and safety. Those internal emotional resources permit the child to ward off threats and dispense with the need to be overly self-protective.[119]

Arthur Combs, a clinical psychologist and Carl Rogers's protégé, developed perceptual psychology, a humanistic approach to the study of persons. His goal was to better understand human experience and behavior in the relationship between the two. I utilized Dr. Combs's theoretical, humanistic-based model of teacher-student (child) relationship for my doctoral thesis and explored his most salient idea: the self as instrument. Such a concept emphasizes the uniqueness of each individual and the reality that each parent is, above all else, a person. Parents, just like professionals, must maintain a positive self-worth and a sense of self-compassion.

Combs differentiated between the scholar and the practitioner. The latter—i.e., the parent—relies on their own intuition, personal data, subjectivity, and emotional understanding of their child. Thus, in the parent-child interpersonal relationship, we can view the mother and father as instruments. All social and emotional responsivity perceived by the child emanates from the parent's own self-experience. As such, the parent's self-esteem and capacity to read their child's cues and respond in a sensitive, compassionate manner as a genuine, congruent person are essential.[120]

A parent who engages their child with responsive, sensitive parenting will greatly improve their child's capacity to thrive as a socially, emotionally, and overall, psychologically healthy child—and later, adult. This occurs for two primary reasons:

Responsive, sensitive parenting is the best practice model to satiate your child's affect hunger.

Responsive, sensitive parenting is the best practice model to ensure that your child internalizes the essential psychological resources of empathy, develops a capacity to play, develops a conscience, and receives significant brain stimulation.

CHAPTER 7

Intersubjectivity: Overview

"In the end is the Word, and the Word is Man—and the Word is with Men."
— JOHN STEINBECK, NOBEL BANQUET SPEECH

THE PREVIOUS SIX chapters feature one underlying concept: intersubjectivity. A term originally coined by the philosopher Edmund Husserl (1859–1938), intersubjectivity is the interchange of thoughts and feelings, both conscious and unconscious, between two persons or "subjects," as facilitated by empathy.

The APA dictionary defines intersubjectivity as follows:

The sharing of subjective experience between two or more people. Intersubjectivity is seen as essential to language and the production of social meaning. The term is often applied to the relationship between a client and a therapist.

Intersubjectivity is interrelational. It is, in philosopher Martin Buber's words, "human to human living, within genuine mutual dialogue."

Today's psychologists are finally exploring intersubjectivity. Until recently, many psychological and psychoanalytic theories focused solely on the individual. Such an approach is known as solipsism, which the APA dictionary defines as follows:

The philosophical position that one can be sure of the existence of nothing outside the self, as other people and things may be mere figments of one's own consciousness. Although psychologically unacceptable, such a position is notoriously difficult to refute, either logically or empirically. The question posed by solipsism has been put in various ways, but all arise from the fact that one's experience of one's own consciousness and identity is direct and unique, so that one is cut off from the same kind of experience of other minds and the things of the world.

Solipsism and intersubjectivity are firmly grounded in specific philosophical principles and are associated with historical time periods. Solipsism, a concept which dates back to Classical Greece, underlies the analytical approaches to the therapist-patient relationship. Intersubjectivity, on the other hand, is associated with philosophy's Continental School, which arose in Western Europe in the nineteenth century.

Why now, after so many centuries, are psychologists emphasizing intersubjectivity?

First, today's zeitgeist reflects the social nature of individuals in relationship with each other. Even the field of psychoanalysis has realized that focusing solely on the patient as an isolated ego is outdated and not therapeutic. Psychoanalysis has shifted to the theory that the therapist, the "other" person, must be considered within the context of social interactions. It's the relationship itself, between therapist and patient, through which healing occurs. The therapist serves as more than a passive reflector or interpreter of the patient's unconscious and ego content. The encounter is mutual.

Second, neuroscience provides empirical evidence of our innate emotional nature and need at birth to engage in mutual social interactions. Such findings validate our inherently biopsychosocial core nature.

Third, the newer Theory of Mind, which has been widely accepted across disciplines, postulates that other people have intentions, desires, beliefs, perceptions, and emotions different than our own. Neuroscience reveals that we share meaning and experiences with others—the antithesis of solipsism. It states that, in turn, a given person in relationship with the "other" will be affected by the other person's actions, emotions, and behaviors. Such a theory has been applied to child development. Thus, how a child develops is studied now in the context of social relationships, and as mentioned above, evidence shows that healthy human development is driven by innate motives for affectivity and ongoing interactions within mutual relationships.

Contemporary psychology has become more scientific *and* significantly more interdisciplinary. Integration of research findings can be found across and within many interrelated fields, branches, and specialties. Examples include neuropsychology, evolutionary psychology, developmental neuroscience, affective neuroscience, neurophilosophy, intersubjective oncology, neuroanthropology, social anthropology, physical anthropology, ethnology, and linguistic anthropology. Most of those specialized and interdisciplinary fields didn't exist during my education and training. An abundance of new data helps us better understand the human being as influenced by a multitude of internal, external, and evolutionary factors.

In the following chapters, we'll take a closer look at intersubjectivity within psychology and neuroscience. Then we'll discuss the understanding of psychic pain through an amalgam of neuroscience and psychology, both of which contribute a significant amount of original scientific research, empirical evidence, and conceptual formulations to our understanding of intersubjectivity. Their boundaries are porous.

CHAPTER 8

Psychology and Intersubjectivity

". . . Deep understanding is, I believe, the most precious gift one can give to another."

— CARL ROGERS

WE PSYCHOTHERAPISTS SELDOM know the long-term results of our efforts. I can recall one case, however, that proved an exception.

A twenty-four-year-old woman named Carolyn came to see me for marital issues. She had three children—ages six, four, and two—and was separated from her husband Joe, who had filed for divorce.

"I'm in a really bad place," Carolyn said during our first therapy interview. "I'm unemployed, have no degrees or vocational skills, and now have to be a twenty-four/seven full-time mother without my children's father. Just before Joe left, we had agreed that he would watch the kids one night a week and that I would start college classes."

"Maybe you still can do that."

"I'd have to ask my parents to babysit. They have already given me so much help."

I was impressed by this young mother's intellect, composure, and motivation to pursue an education. She had an infectious smile and showed great concern for her children.

"What subjects or fields interest you?" I asked.

"I was always good in math in high school, and I like business."

Carolyn and I worked together for more than a year until her divorce was finalized. During that time, she completed two evening classes at the local community college.

At our last session, Carolyn told me, "I think I'm ready to stop coming. You've helped me a lot. The only thing I can't stop thinking about is that I'll be a bag lady and homeless."

"Carolyn," I said, "if you ever become a bag lady—and you won't—you'll be walking around with Nordstrom's bags."

About twenty-five years later, I saw Carolyn in a mall parking lot. Our cars faced each other as we approached them.

She noticed me and waved.

"Hi, Carolyn," I said. "It's been a long time."

She stepped closer and began to bring me up to speed on her life. "I got remarried, Dr. Ruff. I got my bachelor's degree in math and business and then went on to get an MBA. I'm an executive at FSB, an international tech firm, here in the suburbs. Donnie, my oldest son, is married. He and Laura both graduated college. And Sam, my youngest, is a senior in college."

Carolyn looked and sounded joyful—for good reasons, obviously—and I savored the moment. At least one person was living a more fulfilled life as a result of our work together. Before she got into her car, she met my gaze, smiled, and held up her Nordstrom holiday-season shopping bag. She remembered.

Carl Rogers

Carl Ransom Rogers (January 8, 1902–February 4, 1987), who had a foundational influence on my work because I was taught by his students, was the founder of Client-Centered Therapy, now known as Person-Centered Therapy. Rogers is considered one of the founding fathers of psychotherapy. Along with Abraham Maslow, Rogers led a movement known as humanistic psychology. He pioneered clinical research in psychology and was the first major psychologist to videotape and record his counseling sessions with clients. His methods provided valuable clinical data for training therapists and those conducting extensive psychotherapy research. His unusual approach—few psychologists practiced therapy *and* conducted clinical research simultaneously—served as a rewarding, practical means for students like me to gain attunement, self-awareness, and increased empathy via the therapeutic process. For his groundbreaking research platform and methodology, Rogers received the APA Award for Distinguished Scientific Contributions in 1956.

Researchers and therapists initially developed and utilized Rogers's person-centered approach within the fields of psychotherapy and counseling. In time, his unique approach to human relationships received wide acceptance and application in education, group settings, governments, and various professional fields. In a comprehensive study, Stephen J. Haggbloom and colleagues assessed Rogers as the sixth-most eminent psychologist of the twentieth century and second among clinicians only to Sigmund Freud. And a survey conducted in 1982 among 422 US and Canadian psychologists established Rogers as the most influential psychotherapist in history.

The life and principles of Carl Rogers have always been a natural fit for me. His calm, reassuring, and compassionate nature greatly influenced me; I felt we shared similar personalities. And his humanistic, existential, and phenomenological perspective on the theory of intersubjectivity and the human experience proved likewise consistent with my own beliefs and comfort level. By conducting pioneering research in psychotherapy and practicing psychotherapy concurrently, Rogers demonstrated that the two areas are compatible. To this day, research continues to validate his core ideas of unconditional positive regard and accurate empathic understanding of the therapist or "other" in the intersubjective relationship of congruence.

Although I never met Carl Rogers, I've considered him a significant presence throughout my professional career. Several people he trained as first-generation Rogerians at the University of Chicago Counseling Center immersed me in his approach, and those former students became my mentors, professors, supervisors, and private practice associates. I was surrounded by Rogerians, so it only follows that some of his ideas rubbed off on me.

Rogers developed his person-centered therapy in the 1940s. His therapeutic approach is based on his conviction that all human beings strive to fulfill their potential and have the capacity to do so. While becoming one of the first psychologists

CHAPTER 8: PSYCHOLOGY AND INTERSUBJECTIVITY

to focus on the intersubjective relationship between therapist and client, Rogers maintained a firm belief in our innate capacity to develop in a positive and prosocial manner if treated with respect and trust by another person. He believed that people are basically good, and he conceptualized that heredity, early development, environmental and societal factors, and an innate desire for social and emotional growth throughout the lifespan influence each person. Interpersonal connection, he posited, has a positive effect on the growth and wellbeing of both client and therapist, and everything is dependent on the quality of that intersubjective relationship.

According to Rogers, three attributes of the therapist form the core components of the therapeutic relationship: congruence, unconditional positive regard (UPR), and accurate empathic understanding.[121] Rogers in particular and psychotherapy in general contributed the initial and primary conceptual framework later adopted for the more general, non-therapeutic application of the term intersubjectivity. Thus, a genuine, person-to-person intersubjective dialogue or bond requires the following characteristics:

- **Congruence:** Of the three attributes, Rogers considers congruence the most important. Congruence implies that the therapist is genuine, open, and integrated within the therapeutic relationship. The therapist doesn't present a façade; their internal and external experiences are one and the same. In short, the therapist is authentic. Such authenticity functions as a model of a human being struggling toward greater realness. However, Rogers's concept of congruence doesn't imply that only a fully congruent or self-actualized therapist can be effective in counseling.[122] Since therapists are also human, they can't be expected to be fully authentic. Instead, the person-centered model assumes that if therapists are congruent in the relationship with the client, then the process of therapy will commence. Congruence exists on a continuum rather than on an all-or-nothing basis.

- **Unconditional positive regard (UPR):** UPR refers to the therapist's deep and genuine caring for the client. The therapist might not approve of some of the client's actions, but the therapist *does* approve of the client. In short, the therapist presents an attitude of unconditional acceptance. According to Rogers, research indicates that the greater the degree of caring, accepting, and valuing of the client in a non-possessive way, the higher the potential for successful therapy. However, it's impossible for therapists to always feel genuinely caring and accepting.[123]
- **Accurate empathic understanding:** The third and final attribute, accurate empathic understanding refers to the therapist's ability to understand sensitively and accurately—but not sympathetically—the client's experience and feelings in the here-and-now. Empathic understanding implies that the therapist will sense the client's feelings as if they were their own without becoming lost in those feelings.[124] Rogers writes the following:

If I am truly open to the way life is experienced by another person, if I can take his or her world into mine, then I risk seeing life in his or her way . . . and of being changed myself, and we all resist change. Since we all resist change, we tend to view the other person's world only in our terms, not in his or hers. Then we analyze and evaluate it. That's human nature. We do not understand their world. But when the therapist does understand how it truly feels to be in another person's world, without wanting or trying to analyze or judge it, then the therapist and the client can truly blossom and grow in that climate.[125]

Parents and caregivers can use the central concepts and overall intersubjective approach of Rogers's person-centered therapy as a guide to practice responsive, sensitive care. Such therapy exemplifies the necessary attributes and attitude of the caregiver and the atmosphere necessary for the child to feel safe and to grow.

The above core characteristics are as essential within the mother-infant, parent-child, or caregiver-child relationship as they are in a therapeutic therapist-client setting. Such attributes must occur within any genuine meeting. For Rogers, one's inner experiencing is the core concept of self-change. Caring facilitation shown by the parent or caregiver allows the child to gain a unique identity, a greater sense of self-acceptance, and perceived freedom and ownership.

The primary contributions of intersubjectivity and positive child development derive from theories of psychotherapy and philosophy. This is especially the case in person-centered therapy. The core tenets can be employed by parents and caregivers in their own interactions with infants, toddlers, children, adolescents, and adults. Rogers's humanistic and interpersonal approach can be used in any setting outside of the professional therapist's office.

The three core attributes required of the caregiver are the same that Rogers requires of the therapist: congruence, unconditional positive regard, and accurate empathic understanding. Such attributes are critical because they help the caregiver develop a safe, accepting, and trusting interpersonal climate for the child. This, in turn, permits openness and allows a child to self-reflect on their own experiences and to grow emotionally. Within this intersubjective serve and return and genuine dialogue, growth occurs not only in the child but likewise in the parent or caregiver.

Responsive, sensitive care within this intersubjective, person-centered model is an ongoing process. It begins at birth, and the infant will continue the process of becoming a whole, fully functioning, and congruent person throughout their lifetime. There is no destination, but the quality and continuity of intersubjective encounters must continue to permit positive social and emotional development. The child's hunger for affect finds expression in this bilateral mother-child attachment, and this ongoing responsive, sensitive care permits the infant to develop a self, born in intersubjectivity.

Congruence

Your ability as a parent or caregiver to respond to your infant and child in a highly attuned, empathic manner is vital in providing responsive, sensitive parenting. Such a skill functions like radar and allows you to key into the inner emotional world of lived experience within your child. The more accurately you understand your child's emotions, uniqueness, and internal sense of their world, the more accurately your own affective reactions will match the immediate needs and signals of your child. This allows you to be congruent. Your accurate matching of experiencing and awareness demonstrates to your child a sense of safety, nurturance, and synchrony. He or she can trust that you truly know and understand them. The more attuned you become to the verbal and nonverbal cues, sounds, and signals of your child, the more you'll intuitively feel what your child is feeling. Your congruency will become more noticeable to your child as he or she is reassured that your sensitive, social, and emotional actions and responses are genuine. Thus your outer behaviors and affectivity sensed by your child will match your inner experience of your child's needs. This increasingly authentic relationship will continue to be refined throughout the intersubjective relationship. "Unless this congruence is present to a considerable degree," Rogers wrote in 1961, "it is unlikely that significant learning can occur."[126]

Unconditional Positive Regard
Granting your child unconditional positive regard means accepting your child regardless of their behavior. It means that your child senses that you will love, value, and care for them just as they are. Your love and positive responsiveness are not conditional on satisfying the needs or demands of the caregiver. The child feels unjudged, worthy, and fully free to behave authentically. Sometimes you'll disapprove of your child's behavior, but your child won't feel compelled to perform in a certain manner in order to feel like you value them.[127]

Martin Buber

Born in Vienna, Martin Buber was a European philosopher whose thinking and prodigious writings place him in the highest echelon of scholarship. Recognized as one of the most important philosophers of the modern era, he became most widely known after publication of his seminal book, *I and Thou*.[128] While his work has greatly influenced psychology and psychotherapy, his ideas also informed anthropology, sociology, communication theory, economics, education, ethics, family science, family therapy, feminism, Christianity, literary theory and analysis, philosophy, political science, and religious studies. He was multilingual in twelve languages: fluent in German, Hebrew, Yiddish, Polish, English, French, and Italian, and could read Spanish, Dutch, Greek, and Latin.

Course of Study

Buber led his personal life in accordance with his philosophy of dialogue. His approach was based on humanism, phenomenology, and lived experience in the moment. Buber referred to himself as a philosophical anthropologist.

Encyclopedia Britannica Online defines philosophical anthropology as follows:

> *Philosophical anthropology is the discipline within philosophy that seeks to unify the several empirical investigations of human nature to understand individuals as creatures of their environment and creators of their values.*

Max Scheler built the initial philosophical foundation for

philosophical anthropology as a discipline in 1920. Scheler defined the human not so much as a "rational animal," as had been the case since Aristotle, but as a loving being.

Thus, philosophers who explore substantive issues of human nature now prefer to call themselves philosophical anthropologists. Their humanistic and relational orientation distinguishes them from the traditional, widely held, scientifically based empirical approaches inherent in classical and more modern philosophies.

Regardless of the terminology used—for example, "philosophy of physics" versus "philosophical anthropology"—philosophies that maintain a narrow focus employ scientific methodologies to study a particular area, such as physics. Those who espouse the broader, substantive area of human nature refer to themselves as philosophical anthropologists. Their perspective is nonscientific—a discussion of the mind and soul—and explores more spiritual subject matter. Moreover, they focus on social relationships, interhuman domain, and otherness, whereas the scientific, rational philosophers are more solipsistic and study the individual person as a unified self. (Britannica Online.)

Relational Ontology

Buber's central contribution, his philosophy of dialogue, is based on his ontological premise that "all real living is meeting." Buber believed that the essence of being human is interrelatedness. Maurice Friedman, a scholar and Buber's biographer and close friend, wrote, "the fundamental fact of human existence is man with man, the genuine dialogue between man and man." Thus, "to be is to be relational."

The essence of being human, Buber emphasized, is to engage in genuine meeting or dialogue through social relationships. He didn't like being labeled as a "philosopher" or "theologian" and focused on personal experience, not ideas. His core concept of lived experience is grounded in intersubjectivity.[129]

"A person only gains an 'essential self,'" Buber noted, by participating in an actuality "that is neither merely a part of him nor merely outside of him." Intersubjectivity is therefore a human space between two subjects that can neither control nor manipulate. Again, such a claim contrasts sharply with prior analytic philosophies based on an individual self or solipsism.

I-Thou

I and Thou (1923), Buber's most influential philosophical work, is based on a distinction between two word pairs that designate two basic modes of existence: I-Thou (Ich-Du in German) and I-It (Ich-Es). The I-Thou relation is the pure encounter of one unique entity with another in such a way that the other is known without being subsumed under a universal. Not yet subject to classification or limitation, the Thou is not reducible to spatial or temporal characteristics. In contrast, the I-It relation is driven by categories of "same" and "different" and focuses on universal definition. An I-It relation experiences a detached thing, fixed in space and time, while an I-Thou relation participates in the dynamic, living process of an "other."

Buber characterizes I-Thou relations as "dialogical" and I-It relations as "monological." Monologue, Buber explains, isn't just a turning away from the other but also a turning back on oneself (Rückbiegung). It means seeing the other as a classified and hence predictable and manipulable object that exists only as a part of one's own experiences. In contrast, in an I-Thou relation, both participants exist as polarities of relation, whose center lies in the between (Zwischen).

The I of man differs in both modes of existence. The I can be taken as the sum of its inherent attributes and acts, or it can be taken as a singular, whole, irreducible being. The I of the I-It relation is a self-enclosed, solitary individual (der Einzige) that sees itself as the subject of experience. The I of the I-Thou relation is a whole, focused, singular person (der Einzelne) that knows itself as subject. In later writings, Buber clarified that inner life is not exhausted by these two modes of being, but when man presents himself to the world, he takes up one of them.

Buber's basic thesis is that the human being is fundamentally relational. In other words, there can be no I without another person. We exist only in relationship with another person. We gain and develop our own self through intersubjective relationships. "There is no solipsism, only intersubjectivity," Buber stated. "When we suffer in pain, it is always in relation to another." The Internet Encyclopedia of Philosophy elaborates further:

We realize that we always exist in the presence of other selves, and that the self is a part of reality only insofar as it is relational.

In contrast to the traditional philosophic answers to "What is man?" that fixate on reason, self-consciousness or free will, Buber argues that man is the being who faces an "other" and a home is built from relations of mutual confirmation.

I-It

In contrast to the I-Thou relationship, which encourages dialogue, the I-It relationship produces a monologue. While physically near one another, those in an I-It relationship don't experience an intersubjective, mutual meeting among two singular human beings. Indeed, they don't actually meet or bond. The I relates to the other human as an object, a mental representation, an idea within the mind. In such a superficial relationship, the I, consciously or unconsciously, views the other as a commodity or singular entity for self-gain. The other exists only as a cognition. As such, the idea of the other is only a relationship within oneself. Without any sense of mutuality, the encounter becomes a monologue, not a dialogical meeting. Buber sums up "I-It" by saying, "It refers to the world as we experience it."

While a person might strive to engage in mutual, genuine I-Thou meetings, Buber points out, such relationships are rather infrequent. For the most part, human beings tend to engage in more expedient I-It relationships. Buber contends that a correlation exists between human isolation, alienation, dehumanization, and social disconnection and the increase in using people merely as objects and commodities. Such a dynamic reflects the increasingly fast-paced, analytical, materialistic culture of modern existence. Buber believed that increases in I-It relationships not only "devalues existents, but the meaning of all existence."[130]

Core Elements of Genuine Dialogue

Central to Buber's philosophy of dialogue is his belief in the wholeness and uniqueness of the human being within the I-Thou relationship. It is direct, mutual, present, and honest. Buber isn't concerned with what occurs within the minds of the two partners in the I-Thou meeting. What matters instead is what occurs *between* them. Buber rejected the modern-day psychological supposition that the reality of the human-to-human relationship rests within an individual psyche. "The inmost growth of the self does not take place, as people like to suppose today, through our relationship to ourselves," he wrote, "but through being made present by the other and knowing that we are made present by him."[131]

Unlike previous philosophers and psychologists, Buber didn't categorize the human experience according to opposites: inner and outer, subjective and objective, individualistic and collectivistic. Instead, he argued for the interhuman: the ontological dimension in the meeting between persons.[132]

As discussed, genuine dialogue for Buber involves opening oneself to the "otherness" of the other person in the I-Thou relationship. For this to occur, one must truly experience the other side. If not, then the communication is a monologue. That is, the other person is merely an object or content of one's experience. As Buber wrote, "Whenever one lets the other exist only as part of oneself, dialogue becomes a fiction, the mysterious intercourse between two human worlds only a game, and in the rejection of the real life confronting him the essence of all reality begins to disintegrate."[133]

For Buber, intersubjectivity is human-to-human living. His philosophy of authentic dialogue is grounded in humanism and the lived experience or encounter. An intersubjective dialogue can only be genuine and mutually beneficial if both parties engage in certain basic steps, and it requires becoming attuned to one another.[134]

Confirmation

According to Buber, confirmation occurs when a person is confirmed in their uniqueness and potential. Confirmation involves the dynamic between two people, but it goes beyond the interpersonal. Friedman elaborates further:

> *The confirmation of the other must include an actual experiencing of the other side of the relationship so that one can imagine quite concretely what another is feeling, thinking, and knowing. This "inclusion," or "imagining the real," does not abolish the basic distance between oneself and the other. It is rather a bold swinging over into the life of the person one confronts, through which alone I can make that person present in his or her wholeness, unity, and uniqueness.*[135]

The Narrow Ridge

Friedman described Buber's life as a "life of dialogue." Buber exemplified his philosophy of dialogue in his own life. His life was an ongoing, open exploration of the wholeness and uniqueness of what it means to be human. He articulated his perspective on dialogue as follows:

> *I have occasionally described my standpoint to my friends as the "narrow ridge." I wanted by this to express that I did not rest on the broad upland of a system that includes a series of sure statements about the absolute, but on a rocky ridge between the gulfs where there is no sureness of expressible knowledge but the certainty of meeting what remains undisclosed.*

Friedman, Steven Littlejohn, and Karen Foss further emphasize that Buber's philosophy is rooted deeply in lived experience of the moment:

> *Walking on the narrow ridge entails a continual resistance to generalizations, universalities, and categories that obscure the irreducible uniqueness of the Other. Walking on the narrow ridge means carefully managing what are usually understood as opposites, such as freedom and constraint, individuality and community.*[136]

Argentinian writer Jorge Luis Borges saw something in Buber's writings that transcended philosophy:

> *I remember having read, some thirty years ago, the works of Martin Buber and I thought of them as being wonderful poems. And then, when I returned to Buenos Aires, I read a book by a friend of mine. And I found, in its pages, much to my astonishment, that Martin Buber was a philosopher.*

Kenneth Kramer

Kenneth Kramer was a professor emeritus of comparative religious studies at San Jose State University and the author of four books on Martin Buber. In his final book before his passing, *Martin Buber's Dialogue: Discovering Who We Truly Are*,[137] Kramer synthesizes Buber's ideas regarding face-to-face dialogue. He presents four core actions to guide readers toward a mutual dialogical meeting. The four actions, if performed by parents and caregivers, meet the best-practice model of responsive, sensitive parenting. They facilitate the I-Thou meeting through which the infant/child bond is experienced.

- **Turning:** Reorienting your focus from yourself to others as dialogical partners by making them fully present and being made present by them
- **Addressing**: Willingly accepting, affirming, and confirming the other as a dialogical partner, even if disagreeing with their convictions
- **Listening:** Deeply and attentively listening to the other's speaking and boldly (empathically) swinging to their side by imagining their wholeness and unity
- **Responding:** Responsibly answering another's communication by trusting that they, like you, will respond honestly and vulnerably

Kramer separates the four core actions into two distinct pairs. Turning and addressing fall within the first pair, which is all about readiness and the preparatory practices that initiate real dialogue. The second pair includes listening and

CHAPTER 8: PSYCHOLOGY AND INTERSUBJECTIVITY

responding, which facilitate genuine dialogue.

Turning, according to Kramer, isn't just the first action; it's the most essential:

Without mutual turning, there is no dialogue. Turning refers to a double movement: away from all self-preoccupations and distractions and completely, unreservedly toward the other. It is this pivot of one's attention fully toward the other that opens up the dialogic path. Turning occurs when at least one of the dialogical partners reorients their direction of movement away from the self and fully (body/mind spirit) toward the other. Genuine dialogue becomes a possibility when we are able to suspend our focus from what we are doing to the other person's interests and intentions. It is almost as simple as changing your physical position so that you are more able to shift your body into a direct face-to-face encounter with the other person.

Kramer sees addressing, meanwhile, as an extension of turning. It requires a respectful exchange of ideas:

Addressing takes turning farther. It involves the art of becoming fully respectful of the other and in the process of opening up the space for the other to become fully present to you. Addressing occurs when each of the dialogue partners cooperatively accepts the personhood of the other, and then no matter race or culture, gender, age, health or handicap, affirms the other's right to their own opinions, viewpoints, attitudes, or beliefs, even when different from one's own. We address one another through meaningful speech in which we honestly present ourselves.

Listening, Kramer points out, requires the listener to extend empathy and cooperation to the other:

By listening, Buber does not just mean active listening. Far deeper, dialogic listening includes the ability to empathically swing to the other's side and think, feel, and experience what they are thinking, feeling, and experiencing. Listening occurs when each of the dialogue partners hears cooperatively and listens deeply to what is actually said, as well as silences and pauses. Listening is aided by a simple question: "Did you mean that?" Or, "Would you please say what you mean in a different way?" Or, "Is this what you mean?"

Kramer sees responding, the culmination of the four-step process, as an act of courage and total honesty:

Responding is the fruition of the process. Nothing is withheld. One engages the other both responsibly and honestly, courageously risking one's self-image, creatively asking inventive questions, and curiously following provocative levels. Responding occurs when each of the partners cooperatively answers the other person by taking a stand, by speaking in a responsible way honestly, courageously, and without leaving anything out.

CHAPTER 9

Affective Neuroscience and Intersubjectivity

"The capabilities of young children are complex, and the role of intersubjectivity in the developmental process is central."

— COLWYN TREVARTHEN

THE EMERGENCE OF neuroscience as a specialized discipline makes it possible to assess the influence of behavior and emotions on the way the brain functions. Thus, prior formulations regarding the influences of parental and environmental factors on a child's emotional and cognitive development can be scientifically measured. Scientists are rapidly identifying the precise brain location and the qualitative and quantitative effects of such factors, both short term and long term.

So how new is the field of neuroscience? The answer might surprise you. Alcmaeon of Croton, a Presocratic Greek philosopher and medical writer who lived in the sixth century BC, is often referred to as the father of neuroscience. He was the first ancient scholar to posit that the human brain is the primary organ in our body and is connected with the sensory organs. Such a theory was conceivable, he wrote, based on the presence of the optic nerve. Alcmaeon formulated encephalocentrism, a theory that holds that the mind can be found in the brain. His prodigious, far-reaching neurological conceptualizations remain generally accurate to this day.[138]

In chapter 4, we introduced Jaak Panksepp, the founding father of affective neuroscience. Panksepp, an Estonian-born American physiological psychologist, coined the term affective neuroscience, which is also known as social affective neuroscience. The APA dictionary defines the specialty as follows:

A discipline that addresses the brain mechanism's underlying emotions. In seeking to understand the particular roles of major subcortical and cortical structures in the elicitation, experience, and regulation of emotion, affective neuroscience provides an important framework for understanding the neural processes that underlie psychopathology, particularly the mood and substance-related disorders.[139]

Until the late 1990s, the study of cognition excluded emotion and focused on non-emotional processes (e.g. memory, attention, perception, action, problem-solving, and mental imagery). As a result, the respective study of the neural basis of non-emotional and emotional processes emerged as two separate fields: cognitive and affective neuroscience. The distinction between non-emotional and emotional processes is now thought to be

CHAPTER 9: AFFECTIVE NEUROSCIENCE AND INTERSUBJECTIVITY

largely artificial, since the two types of process often involve overlapping neural and mental mechanisms. Thus, when we use cognition's broadest definition, affective neuroscience could also be called the cognitive neuroscience of emotion.

Weighing in at around three pounds, the human brain is far more powerful than the most powerful computer. Every second, the brain processes hundreds of billions of bits of information. The brain's one hundred billion neurons send signals that allow us to communicate, make plans, solve problems, detect threats, protect ourselves, and remember the world around us. When brain functions are altered, mental health and neurological disorders arise. Irregular brain function can affect judgment, communication, emotions, behavior, and our understanding of reality.

Here are a few things you might not know about the human brain:

- 60% of the brain is made up of fat; it is one of the fattiest organs in the body.
- The human brain can generate approximately twenty-three watts of power when awake.
- The brain receives 20% of the total blood and oxygen produced in our body.
- Blood vessels in the brain run almost 100,000 miles in length.
- In early pregnancy, the embryo's brain creates 250,000 new neurons per minute.
- In the first few years of life, more than one million new neural connections form every second.

- The human brain consists of one hundred billion neurons and over one hundred trillion synaptic connections.
- There are more neurons in a single brain than stars in the Milky Way.[140]

Recent neuroscientific research shows that babies have as many neurons as adults and that stimulation is necessary to form connections between them for growth and learning. Babies are equipped to learn through multisensory experiences.[141]

Chronic Understimulation: A lack of serve and return causes the child to experience affect hunger. If caregivers fail to support a young child's need for cognitive, vocal, social, and emotional engagement, intervention can be helpful. What does chronic understimulation look like? One scenario involves precious few daily interactions that provide opportunities for young children to engage in active conversation with adult caregivers. Another involves frequent periods during which infants or toddlers are left in front of a television for hours at a time. In some cases, the lack of engagement is the result of a limited understanding of the developmental needs of young children. In others, it might be caused by a range of risk factors, such as caregiver depression, social or geographic isolation, the stresses of poverty or discrimination, or a distracting family illness. Understanding the precipitating factors and employing appropriate strategies to address identified needs (e.g. from simple parenting education to enriched learning experiences through high-quality child care or early education programs) can produce strong returns on relatively simple, voluntary interventions.[142]

CHAPTER 9: AFFECTIVE NEUROSCIENCE AND INTERSUBJECTIVITY

Groundbreaking research studies in affective neuroscience focus on innate infant brain architecture and responsive, sensitive care that enables newborns to engage in social interaction from birth onward. In the following sections, we'll explore seminal scientific findings from two eminent pioneers in the neuroscientific study of intersubjectivity: Colwyn Trevarthen and Vittorio Gallese. These two scientists have been instrumental in the advancement of interdisciplinary research. Their work has significantly increased our understanding of the inherent social nature of neonates and their ability to engage in intersubjective relationships.

Colwyn Trevarthen

Currently emeritus professor of child psychology and psychobiology at the University of Edinburgh, UK, Colwyn Trevarthen was born and raised in New Zealand and majored in biology at the Universities of Auckland and Otago. He earned a PhD in psychobiology, the science of the brain, at the California Institute of Technology, where he worked with Roger Sperry on functions of the brain and cognition. At the invitation of Jerome Brunner, in 1966 Trevarthen served as a research fellow at the Center for Cognitive Studies at Harvard University, where he began his research on infants.

Since the 1960s, Colwyn Trevarthen has distinguished himself as perhaps the leading researcher in infant communication and brain development and the emotional health of children. He's best known for his remarkable research on newborns. Wikipedia offers a tidy summation of his work:

[Trevarthen] believes that very young babies rapidly develop proto-cultural intelligence through interacting with other people, including in teasing fun play. For instance, he has demonstrated that a newborn has an innate ability to initiate a dialogic relationship with an adult and then build up this relationship through eye contact, smiling, and other holistic body functions rhythmically and cooperatively.

He studied successful interactions between infants and their primary care givers and found that the mother's responsiveness to her baby's initiatives supported and developed intersubjectivity (shared understanding), which he regarded as the basis of all effective communication, interaction, and learning.

He has applied intersubjectivity to the very rapid cultural development of newborn infants and used the term "primary intersubjectivity" to refer to early developing sensory-motor processes of interaction between infants and caregivers. He believes babies are looking for companionship (including the sense of fun and playfulness), engagement, and relationship (rather than using the term attachment), and that companions can include mothers, fathers, other adults, peers, and siblings; he has said, "I think the ideal companion—and it can be a practitioner or not—is a familiar person who really treats the baby with playful human respect."

In later years his work has focused on the musicality of babies, including its use in communication.

The Self Born in Intersubjectivity

In an article entitled "What is it like to be a person who knows nothing? Defining the active intersubjective mind of a newborn

CHAPTER 9: AFFECTIVE NEUROSCIENCE AND INTERSUBJECTIVITY

human being,"[143] Colwyn Trevarthen summarizes his revolutionary findings as follows:

As thinking adults depend upon years of practical experience, reasoning about facts and causes, and language to sustain their knowledge, beliefs, and memories, and to understand one another, it seems quite absurd to suggest that a newborn infant has intersubjective mental capacities. But detailed research on how neonatal selves coordinate the rhythms of their movements and senses, and how they engage in intimate and seductive precision with other persons' movements, sensing their purposes and feelings, gives evidence that it is so. The developmental and functional neuroscience of the human brain agrees. Indeed, it seems that cultural intelligence itself is motivated at every stage by the kind of powers of innate intersubjective sympathy that an alert infant can show shortly after birth. We are born to generate shifting states of self-awareness, to show them to other persons, and to provoke interest and affectionate responses from them. Thus starts a new psychology of the creativity and cooperative knowing and meaning in human communities.

We are living in an exciting age! As we gain a deeper understanding of the innate social and emotional nature of the infant, we're discarding long-held beliefs and rewriting the account of the human infant's development.

Parent-infant research studies over the past several decades indicate that the infant experiences different layers of intersubjective attunement in human development before language. Trevarthen has applied intersubjectivity, first identified as innate in the 1970s, to the rapid cultural development of newborns:

- Research suggests that, as babies, humans are biologically wired to coordinate their actions with others.
- This ability to coordinate and sync with others facilitates cognitive and emotional learning through social interaction.
- The most socially productive relationship between children and adults is bidirectional, where both parties actively define a shared culture.
- The bidirectional aspect lets the active parties organize the relationship as they see fit. What they see as important receives the most focus.
- Using intersubjectivity, emphasis is placed on the idea that children are actively involved in how they learn.[144]

Trevarthen's analysis of his empirical data collected since the 1960s indicates definitive stages in the infant's development of intersubjectivity. Significant and progressive contiguous passages prepare the infant to develop and engage in higher-order skills. Areas of competency include communication and thinking, which consist of conversational speech, the creation of narrative explanations, and the sharing of myths, beliefs, and scientific ideas introduced and modeled by the parent's unique culture.

In the following passage, Trevarthen and Stein Bråten explore three layers of intersubjectivity that operate throughout the normal lifespan:

CHAPTER 9: AFFECTIVE NEUROSCIENCE AND INTERSUBJECTIVITY

The primary intersubjective dialogues *of protoconversation in reciprocal sympathetic imitation exhibited in first weeks of life lead to more lively jokes and games with any motions of "other" awareness. Initiatives are tested in the teasing and provocative way. Affectionate attachments are strengthened by display and build friendships around habitual "formats" or "rituals" of baby songs and action games in which the infants learn to take an active part, for example, by an eleven-day-old on the nursing table in the dance-like interplay with her mother. An exchange of limitations and expressions of emotion may be elicited in the first hours after birth, for example, the infant showing initiative as well as copying movements, which reveals that imitation to reproduce a movement made by another is but one element in the innate capacity for mutual engagements into expressions of sympathetic interest. The mutual mirroring in turn-taking which we find in the torrent verbal conversation is clearly foreshadowed in these first bouts of sympathetic mimetic play, and the "communicative musicality" entailed in dyadic protoconversation allows it to be captured in terms of the perimeter of musicality such as "pulse" and "quality." After a few months an infant may show a wider sociability, being capable of engaging concurrently with more than one other.*

Secondary intersubjective attunement *is a triangular subject-subject-object format in which objects of joint attention and emotional referencing are brought into play as occurrences of mutual attention within trusting relations of companionship. The infant displays to others of knowledge and skill learned by sharing intentions and interests are animated by emotions of "pride" and "shame." Others' object-oriented acts elicited* *participant perception or reenactment, for example, by infants who learn to reciprocate their caregivers' spoon-feeding before their first birthday, e.g., as recorded by Bråten, and sometimes help-oriented co-movements realizing the other's (failed) intention, as in Trevarthen and Hubley's examples of Tracy, under twelve months, "helping" her mother move an object out of the way. In the final months of the first years the words people use to label people, objects, or actions attract attention and invite imitation. Then after fourteen months or so the gestures and vocalizations of "protolanguage" give way to clear speech. Toddlers soon began to combine words to predicates linguistically, e.g., "Doggy wet," "Ball roll," giving voice to shared topics and meanings found in joint and mutual awareness.*

Tertiary intersubjective understanding *in conversational and narrative speech, entailing prediction and a sense of verbal or narrative self and other in first-order modes of symbolic communication, and (from three to six years) second-order understanding of others' minds and emotions (theory or simulation of mind) opens for perspective-taking and emotional absorption, even in fictional others, for self-other dialoguing in dramas of narrative imagination, for simulation of conversation partners' minds, and for listeners completing the speaker's aborted statements by virtue of other-centered participation.*[145]

Protoconversations are important because they're all about emotion—two people tuning in to each other on an emotional level—which is the foundation for all effective communication. "A protoconversation is an interaction between an adult (typically a mother) and baby that includes words, sounds, and gestures and that attempts to convey meaning before the onset of language in the child."[146] Protoconversation, Trevarthen emphasizes, serves as the infant's emotional foundation, upon which all later stages, whether cognitive or emotional, are layered. A child's social, emotional, cognitive, and neural development depends on responsive, sensitive care during this first stage.

Trevarthen and his research associates identified patterns of communication and styles of interaction, revealing that interpersonal aspects of communication are integral to child development and meaningful learning. Beginning at birth, infants learn through their interactions and relationships. Through these close and lively interactions, young children develop a sense of identity, place, and belonging. The process involves giving and receiving feedback, both verbal and non-verbal, which takes place through any social relationship the child participates in and influences. In one study, Trevarthen showed that even two-month-old infants can initiate social interactions with adults. Trevarthen emphasizes the emotional and psychological processes present in supporting consciousness and thinking in the brain.[147]

In his groundbreaking chapter, "The self born in intersubjectivity: the psychology of an infant communicating," in the book *The Perceived Self: Ecological and Interpersonal Sources of Self-Knowledge*, Trevarthen elucidates the powerful innate capacity of the newborn to respond to others as an interpersonal self:

Communication with persons is possible from birth, and we should not be surprised at this. It is in the nature of human consciousness to experience being experienced: to be an actor who can act in relation to other conscious sources of agency, and to be a source of emotions while accepting the emotional qualities of vitality and feeling from other persons by instantaneous empathy. This interpersonal self, this person who breaks the private integrity of the ecological self, splitting its ego center and reconstituting it as part of a communication dipole or multipole, is fundamental to the human condition.

Nevertheless, our psychological tradition, observing the limited cognitive powers of the newborn and giving great value to the cultivated intelligence of an educated person, has assumed that the mind of an infant is incoherent, with undefined perceptions and incapable of contributing to communication, except to solicit help reflexively for biological functions. On the evidence from development, however, and from other everyday evidence, it would seem that the communicating interpersonal self is the very foundation for the cognitive or thinking self who will grow up to solve problems "in the head." The core of every human consciousness appears to be an immediate, irrational, and verbalized, conceptless, totally atheoretical potential for rapport of the self with another's mind.

Even if the mind of a linguistically sophisticated adult may have an autonomous expertise in the mental recreation of meaningful propositions "in one head" as many philosophers have assumed, this is evidently not the primary condition of our consciousness and thinking. A delicate and immediate with-the-other awareness comes first. Human self-awareness is thus one manifestation of mind in a person who is capable of being a companion and confidant to the responses of the other at an

CHAPTER 9: AFFECTIVE NEUROSCIENCE AND INTERSUBJECTIVITY

emotional level, from birth. Infants communicate and think emotionally.[148]

Trevarthen's research on early infant development focuses on motives and emotions and the psychological nature of an infant's capacity to communicate as a precognitive intersubjective self. He asserts that the motivation to actively engage others is innate. It is a deeply ingrained, prewired part of the evolutionary brain. Trevarthen, remaining true to his roots as a psychologist, seeks to understand those earliest traces of a newborn's self-awareness and what that implies regarding their development as a person. In his holistic or biopsychosocial approach, which is based on lived experiences and subjective emotional responsiveness and sensitivities, Trevarthen studies what it means to be human and the process through which we come to know others and hence ourselves. Such an approach is the antithesis of a behavioristic, rationalistic, or strictly cognitive paradigm.

An infant's emotional experiences and need for affective parent-child serve and return are innate motives and reactions and are therefore preconscious. They occur prior to the onset of cognition and logical thinking in the brain. Indeed, later cognitive motives and neuronal firings are built upon the earliest intersubjective emotional layers of the brain.

The study of motivation and emotion in psychology isn't new, of course. It was my first required course as an undergraduate. That class, taken with Dr. Thompson, was referred to as "Mot and Emot." Today, motivation and emotion still constitute a core required curriculum in the field.

Trevarthen offers examples of the responsive, sensitive mother's essential orientations and supportive behaviors:

When she speaks to her baby, a happy mother's facial expressions are exaggerated and friendly, playful, and affectionate. Her voice assumes a gentle, relaxed, breathy quality, with a singular pitch set high, about 300 Hz. She makes short utterances with spiked, undulating, or gliding pitch contours. These are the defining characteristics of "intuitive motherese," which has been shown to be the same when mothers are speaking different languages.

The hand movements the mother makes as she pats or strokes the baby are gentle, periodic, and with repeating rhythms superimposed. The frequency of this touching gives a clear message of her emotion and sensitivity. Face and head movements, vocalizations, and hand movements are coordinated or synchronized; clearly, they are regulated by one mechanism in the mother that conveys the dynamic motive states of herself as she seeks to have the best communication with her infant.[149]

Emotions in mother-infant communication: The emotional responsivity, attunement, and communications between mother and infant determine the affective and social wellbeing of the neonate. If she can communicate love, nurturance, and safety, a mother will satiate the infant's innate hunger for maternal intersubjective affect.

Vittorio Gallese

Vittorio Gallese, MD, a former professor in experimental aesthetics at the University of London, currently serves as a professor of psychobiology at the University of Parma, Italy. As an expert in neurophysiology, cognitive neuroscience, social neuroscience, and philosophy of mind, he co-discovered mirror neurons. His research attempts to elucidate the functional organization of brain mechanisms responsible for things like social cognition, empathy, and mindreading, and his work has focused on the musicality of babies, including its use in communication. Among his major contributions is the elaboration of a theoretical model of basic aspects of social cognition: Embodied Simulation Theory. He has written three books, edited several others, and published more than two hundred papers in international peer-reviewed journals.

The Mirror Neuron System

Some of the greatest scientific breakthroughs have been made accidentally within a laboratory. That was certainly the case with one of the most significant findings of the twenty-first century: the mirror neuron.

In a neuroscience laboratory in Parma, Italy, in 1991, a monkey sat in a specially designed chair while researchers went to lunch. Wires had been implanted in the region of the monkey's brain associated with planning and carrying out movements. Whenever the monkey grasped and moved an object, cells in that brain region fired. A monitor then registered a sound: *brrrrrip, brrrrrip, brrrrrip*. After lunch, a researcher entered the lab, and the monkey looked at him. When the researcher lifted what remained of his lunch to his lips, the monitor immediately sounded, *brrrrrip, brrrrrip, brrrrrip*. Simultaneously, the researcher observed neurons beginning to fire in the monkey's premotor cortex—the exact same area that indicated activity when the monkey itself made a similar hand movement.

"The discovery of the mirror neurons system provides clear scientific evidence that intersubjective experiences are mapped onto an individual's cerebral functioning from the first years of life," Gallese writes. "The discovery of the mirror neurons system offers a neurological explanation which links the infant/parent bilateral intersubjective emotional responsivity to the brain within the maternal empathy and mirror neuron theory."[150]

In this book, coauthored with Massimo Ammaniti,[151] Gallese focuses on neurobiological circuits and regions stimulated in the brain that are mirrored as maternal empathy when a mother observes her child's face. He writes, "The activity of the frontolimbic system intervenes in modulating social and emotional behavior and affect-regulating functions, which are specifically involved in the attachment system, as we have discovered in our research."

As explored in chapter 6, an infant's responsiveness stems from innate survival needs deeply embedded in the primitive brain. Gallese notes that Darwin stated the importance of the infant's face, which stimulates adults to respond to and care for their child, "increasing infant adaptation, that is, reproductive success, and facilitating survivorship of one's own offspring." He adds, "Subsequently, Konrad Lorenz highlighted that infantile facial features serve as an infant schema with innate releasing mechanisms for affective bond and nurturing in adult humans. Infantile facial features are characterized by a relatively large head, predominance of the brain, large and low-lying eyes, and bulging cheek region.[152] In this regard, Bowlby hypothesized that these 'babyish' features would increase the infant's chance of survival by stimulating parental responses."[153]

The Mirror Mechanism in Humans

Gallese originally studied the activation of mirror neurons in the brains of macaque monkeys. He has since helped to discover the existence of the mirror mechanism (MM) in the human brain. "The MM for action in humans is coarsely somatotopically activated when we execute mouth-, hand-, and foot-related acts," he writes, "and is also activated when we observe the same motor acts executed by others. Watching someone grasping a cup of coffee, biting an apple, or kicking a football activates in our brain the same cortical regions that would be activated if we were doing the same."[154]

The discovery of the MM has greatly influenced neuroscience, psychology, and the social sciences. The mirror neurons are a special category of brain cells that fire when a person performs a motor action and, simultaneously, when the observer, the "other," witnesses someone else making the same movement. This finding has dramatically altered our understanding of the human as a social animal within the context of an intersubjective connection and alterity of the other. It has also affirmed the preeminent role of innate, preconscious affectivity and emotionality of "the self born into intersubjectivity." Such a concept emanates from Trevarthen's discovery of the infant's inherent capacity for social and emotional responsiveness and relationship with their birth mother.

Findings confirm Trevarthen's own data that cognitive, intellectual, and rational thinking occurs *after* the critical early affective and pre-cognitive stages. Moreover, newborns sense their humanness at birth and begin to acquire self-knowledge, self-awareness, and meaning through mimicked, nonverbal, observed, and experienced social interactions. Put more simply, social cognition and empathy precede intellectual development.

Gallese and Ammaniti, like Trevarthen, confirm the occurrence of intersubjectivity in early infant social and emotional development—a finding as critical as the concept of attachment theory. Ammaniti and Gallese propose that the intersubjective motivational system "is like a constant barometer that gives us information about our self and others in different contexts... Intersubjective processes are like a blueprint underneath every motivational system, and in the case of the attachment system, they are activated when attachment needs emerge."[155]

Such a claim reaffirms Buber's concept that "all living is human to human meeting." We discover our unique self only through our genuine and mutual relationships with others. In seeing the face of the other, we enter into intersubjectivity and, at that moment, become an individual self. We maintain distance and uniqueness within this intersubjective, dialogical serve and return. To be otherwise would mean living as a solipsistic, egocentric self.

Embodied Simulation Theory

Gallese is probably best known for his two interconnected areas of research: mirror neurons and embodied simulation theory.

CHAPTER 9: AFFECTIVE NEUROSCIENCE AND INTERSUBJECTIVITY

Embodied simulation (ES) theory is, among other things, a theory of social cognition—a theory of how it is we understand others' actions, intentions, emotions, and sensations. "The fundamental mechanism that allows us a direct experiential grasp of the mind of others," Gallese writes, "is not conceptual reasoning but direct simulation of the observed events through the mirror mechanism." Our core connection to the world and the essence of our humanness stems from our social and affective nature. We understand others of our species through empathy and the firing of our mirror neurons.

> ... *an important aspect of intersubjectivity, when witnessing the expression of others' emotions and sensations, can be described in terms of reuse of the same neural circuits underpinning our own emotional and sensory experience.*[156]
>
> *It has been proposed that a common functional mechanism, embodied simulation (ES), can account for this variety of intersubjective phenomena in an integrated and neurologically plausible way.*[157]

A central tenet of Gallese's ES theory is *intercorporeality*:

> *Intercorporeality is a notion proposed by Merleau-Ponty that enables us to illuminate social understanding in an alternative way, by focusing on the relation between one's own body and that of the other.*[158]

Another important tenet of Gallese's ES theory is *intentional attunement*:

A direct form of understanding others from within, as it were—intentional attunement—is achieved by the activation of neural systems underpinning what we and others do and feel. Parallel to the detached third-person sensory description of the third-person sensory description of the observed social stimuli, internal non-propositional "representations" in bodily format of the body states associated with actions, emotions, and sensations are evoked in the observer, as if he or she were performing a similar action or experiencing a similar emotion or sensation.

The neural circuits activated in a person carrying out actions, expressing emotions, and experiencing sensations are activated also, automatically via a mirror neuron system, in the observer of those actions, emotions, and sensations. It is proposed that this finding of shared activation suggests a functional mechanism of "embodied simulation" that consists of the automatic, unconscious, and non-inferential simulation in the observer of actions, emotions, and sensations carried out and experienced by the observed. It is proposed also that the shared neural activation pattern and the accompanying embodied simulation constitute a fundamental biological basis for understanding another's mind.[159]

ES theory provides a unitary account of basic aspects of intersubjectivity. It shows that people reuse their own mental states or processes represented in bodily format to functionally attribute them to others.

CHAPTER 9: AFFECTIVE NEUROSCIENCE AND INTERSUBJECTIVITY

The Mirror Mechanism: Mirroring Others' Motor Goals and Intentions

Gallese, while exploring the mirror mechanism in more depth, wrote the following description:

> *The Mirror Mechanism (MM) in humans has been shown to be involved in imitation of simple movements, and in imitation learning of complex skills, like learning how to play a guitar. Furthermore, they can offer a neurophysiological explanation of many interesting phenomena described by social psychologists, like the "chameleon effect"—observers' nonconscious mimicry of bodily postures, expressions, and behavior of their social partners. It is worth noting that such examples of nonconscious intersubjective mimesis all share a prosocial character, since their occurrence increases during social interactions with affiliative purposes.*[160]
>
> *The presence of the MM in both nonhuman and human brains presents a new evolutionary scenario, with "motor cognition" as a leading element in the emergence of human intersubjectivity.*[161]
>
> *We don't necessarily need to "metarepresent" in propositional format the intentions of others to understand them. Motor goals and intentions are part of the motor system's vocabulary. Most of the time we don't explicitly ascribe intentions to others; we simply detect them. When witnessing others' behaviors, we can grasp their motor intentional contents without needing to metarepresent them.*[162]

Deirdre Wilson, a British linguist and cognitive scientist, defined metarepresentation as our mind's ability to denote "a higher-order representation with a lower-order representation embedded within." What is an example of metarepresentation in theory of mind? Imagine you observe someone pick up a key and walk with it toward a closed door. Based on your capacity for mental state attribution (and your knowledge of keys and doors), you might reasonably infer that this person intends to unlock the door.[163]

The Shared World of Emotions and Sensations

Gallese expands further on his ES theory:

The perception and production of emotion-related facial expressions could impinge on neural structures whose function can be hypothesized to be similar to the MM. Indeed, observation and imitation of facial expressions activate the same restricted group of brain structures, including the ventral premotor cortex, the insula, and the amygdala. Voluntary imitation of the expressions of emotions, however, doesn't necessarily produce a subjective experience of the emotion we're imitating.

An fMRI study explored this phenomenon by scanning the brain activity of healthy participants experiencing disgust, which was induced by the inhalation of disgusting odorants and the observation of video clips showing other people displaying the same emotion with their facial expressions. Witnessing other people's facial expressions of disgust activates the left anterior insula at the same location activated by the first-person subjective experience of disgust... It appears, therefore, that a centric dimension exists in the experience of a given affective state. When observing someone else's facial expression, we don't understand its meaning only through explicit inference from analogy; the other person's emotion is first and foremost constituted and directly understood by reusing part of the same neural circuits used to capture our first-person experience of the same emotion.

Researchers have used similar mechanisms to describe the perception of pain... Such findings suggest that intersubjectivity can be found in our neural circuitry. Embodied simulation (ES), a common functional mechanism, can account for this variety of intersubjective phenomena and integrated in a biologically plausible way.[164]

Maternal Empathy and The Mirror Neuron System

The neurobiological transformations of the maternal brain during pregnancy and the postnatal period increase the birth mother's capacity to be empathic and more responsive and sensitive to her newborn. It is significant and fascinating that the maternal human brain serves as a corollary for all primary psychological concepts involved in responsive, sensitive parenting discussed in previous chapters. In the following quotation, Gallese succinctly articulates the dramatic influence of his pioneering discoveries of the mirror neuron and embodied simulation theory on the mother's heightened neurobiological capacity to care for her newborn. Additionally, this synopsis serves to illustrate the current interdisciplinary synthesis of knowledge and the porous boundaries between psychology and neuroscience:

Mirror neurons map observed and executed actions, personally experienced in observed emotions, or sensations within the same neural substrate by means of "embodied simulation" processes. This concept of embodiment is used to explain how neurobiological events are sought to account for mental events. By means of "embodied simulation," internal representations of the body states associated with actions, emotions, and sensations are evoked in the observer, as in the case of mothers, as though they would be doing a similar action or experiencing a similar emotion or sensation. These functional processes enhance individuals confronting the behavior of others and experiencing a specific phenomenal state of intentional attunement. Such a condition generates a peculiar quality of familiarity with other individuals, produced by the collapse of the others' intentions and emotions into the observer's. In this way, the Mirror Neurons System (MNS) can be described as the neurobiological correlate of the intersubjective system, since it represents the innate and embodied motivation to be in contact with others' emotions and to share subjective experiences with them.[165]

CHAPTER 10

Psychic Pain and Intersubjectivity

"All pain is one malady with many names."
— Antiphanes, ca. 400 BC

To this day, I still suffer occasional flashbacks. The moment occurred during a family therapy session. I'll never forget the pain, which exceeded anything I've ever experienced as a psychotherapist.

I was sitting with Larry, a sixteen-year-old boy I was treating for depression and disruptive behavior, in an interview room at an acute care psychiatric hospital. We were waiting for his mother to join us for a preliminary family meeting.

"How are you feeling about seeing your mother today?" I asked.

"Scared," Larry answered.

"Why are you scared?"

"Because we don't get along. She blames me for everything.

I can never do anything right. She hates me and loves my little sister."

We heard a knock on the door, and Mrs. Williams entered the room.

"Thank you for coming," I said as soon as she sat down. "Your son is making progress and is off suicide watch. The purpose of our meeting today is to look at your relationship with Larry and any problems we can work on together."

Mrs. Williams, seated directly across from her son, exploded in anger. "You've been a difficult child your whole life. You always want things your way. Even when your father was living with us, you'd never listen. I'm tired of it all. I should've never had you."

I sat in stunned silence. Larry had been ambushed and rejected by his own birth mother. I turned to him and saw that he was crying. He sat motionless with his head down. He was lifeless, in severe pain, and I couldn't help but feel his suffering in my gut. I was witnessing the death of a human soul.

Throughout my five decades of clinical practice, I conducted thousands of comprehensive psychological evaluations. Of the many abnormal personality features I assessed in adolescents, psychic pain proved the most common. It typically correlated with high scores on a specific cluster of diagnostic scales and clinical syndromes, including self-devaluation, body disapproval, peer insecurity, family discord, and childhood neglect, abuse, or trauma. The most frequently co-occurring clinical syndrome associated with psychic pain was depression, which was often accompanied by suicidal ideations.

APA's online dictionary defines psychic pain as follows:

CHAPTER 10: PSYCHIC PAIN AND INTERSUBJECTIVITY

Intolerable pain caused by intense psychological suffering (rather than physical dysfunction). At its extreme, prolonged psychic pain can lead to suicide attempts.

Eliana Tossani, an Italian psychologist, wrote:

In the literature, terms such as mental pain, psychic pain, psychological pain, emptiness, psychache, internal perturbation, and psychological quality of life have been used to refer to the same construct.[166]

In all my years of practice, I have found a consistently high correlation between psychic pain and affect hunger. Their co-occurrence is diagnostic and suggests insufficient responsive care during the formative years of development. It points to the neglect of innate neurochemical, biological, and psychological needs for maternal and paternal affection and interactions. Neglected children function more as solipsistic individuals who are socially and emotionally withdrawn and isolated from others. They lack stimulation, touch, nurturance, soothing, emotionality, safety, and serve and return due to the physical and/or emotional absence of responsive, sensitive caregiving. Deprived of their essential developmental needs and any positive human interactions, they experience rejection and feel alienated from their community. The result is psychic pain.

David Bakan, an American psychologist who passed away in 2004, noted that "the individual feels psychological pain the moment he/she becomes separated from a significant other."

Bakan believed that pain is "the person's tendency toward maintaining individual psychological wholeness and social unity."[167] Colwyn Trevarthen, meanwhile, observed that the mother is the child's first companion. And Martin Buber noted that the mother provides the child's first I-Thou relationship. When the initial and essential intersubjective emotional foundation is absent, a child experiences psychic pain.

After Larry's mother left, he remained motionless and unresponsive. I walked him back to his room and placed him on an intensive suicide watch in direct eye contact with the nursing station. Mrs. Williams did not attend the subsequent treatment team meeting nor even respond to my phone call. Our social worker contacted Child and Family Services (CFS), who came and interviewed Larry a few days later. He was off suicide watch and his mood had improved, and he told them that he wanted to go home. However, this was not an option. Prior to meeting with Larry, the case worker had met with Larry's mother. She informed the CFS staff member that she wanted to give up custody of Larry.

A week after Larry met with Child and Family Services at the hospital, he was discharged to a CFS caseworker and placed in a temporary foster home. Per our treatment plan recommendation, arrangements were made for him to immediately attend a therapeutic day treatment program. This program would give Larry the more intensive, structured treatment setting he required, along with school and psychiatric and medication evaluation.

I did not see Larry again after he left the hospital. However, the discharge summary from the day treatment program noted that Larry's level of psychological functioning had significantly improved and that his dosage of antidepressant medicant had been decreased. The CFS had also made arrangements for Larry to live with a paternal uncle out of state.

Larry's case illustrates the longing for the mother even on the part of a child who has been totally rejected by her. It also demonstrates the importance of the mental healthcare infrastructure and of other family members in rehabilitating such children and giving them a chance at a good life.

Interaction Between Social Pain and Physical Pain

In a groundbreaking study, a team led by psychologist Ethan Kross revealed that physical pain and intense feelings of social rejection "hurt" in the same way.[168] Why is this so? Because, as the group's key finding shows, "the same regions of the brain that become active in response to painful sensory experiences are activated during intense periods of social rejection." Kross's group was the first to establish a neural overlap between the experiences of physical pain and social rejection. Naomi Eisenberger and Matthew Lieberman offer the following description of pain overlap theory:

Pain overlap theory proposes that social pain, the pain that we experience when social relationships are damaged or lost, and physical pain, the pain that we experience upon physical injury, share parts of the same underlying processing system. When people feel emotional pain, the same areas of the brain get activated as when people feel physical pain: the anterior insula and the anterior cingulate cortex.[169]

Ming Zhang et al. view pain overlap as an evolutionary adaptation:

There is reason to believe that pain overlap occurred as an evolutionary survival need. The risk of damage to social relationships and physical damage were threats to human survival during evolution, during the time when it was very important to respond to these threats in a timely manner. It is well known that the pain system related to physical injury formed in the early stages of human evolution. However, social life gradually became more and more important for people's survival during the course of human civilization. The detection of social threats, therefore, developed in relation to the same functional system. People's reactions to social and physical pain may overlap and interfere with each other. In fact, there is evidence to support these opinions.[170]

Jaak Panksepp offers this further interesting perspective on pain overlap theory:

Because of the prolonged period of immaturity and the critical need for maternal care in mammalian infants, it has been suggested that the pain mechanisms involved in detecting and preventing physical danger were co-opted by the more recently evolved social attachment system to detect and prevent social separation.[171]

Brief Synopsis of Kross's Experiment

The study involved forty people who had experienced a romantic breakup within the past six months that had caused them to

CHAPTER 10: PSYCHIC PAIN AND INTERSUBJECTIVITY

feel rejected. Each subject completed two tasks. One was related to feelings of rejection, the other to sensations of physical pain in the body.

The experimental research design was as follows:

During the rejection task, participants viewed a photo of their ex-partner and thought about how they felt during their breakup, or they viewed a photo of a friend and thought about a recent positive experience they'd had with that person. During the physical pain task, researchers attached a thermal stimulation device to each participant's left forearm. During some trials, the probe delivered a painful but tolerable stimulation akin to holding a hot cup of coffee. During other trials, it delivered non-painful, warm stimulation.

Participants performed their tasks while undergoing functional magnetic resonance imaging (fMRI) scans. The researchers analyzed the fMRI scans, focusing on the whole brain and on various regions of interest identified in earlier studies of physical pain. They also compared the study's results to a database of more than 500 previous fMRI studies of brain responses to physical pain, emotion, working memory, attention switching, long-term memory, and interference resolution.[172]

Kross summarized the findings as follows:

We found that powerfully inducing feelings of social rejection activates regions of the brain that are involved in physical pain sensation, which are rarely activated in neuroimaging studies of emotion. These findings are consistent with the idea that the experience of social rejection, or social loss more generally, may represent a distinct emotional experience that is uniquely associated with physical pain.

We use the words *hurt* and *pain* to refer to our experience of both physical pain and social rejection.

Shared Neural Circuit of Physical Pain and Social Pain

Evidence from behavioral responses supports the hypothesis that social pain and physical pain interfere with the perception of one when the other is present. In fact, behavioral performance stems from the fact that social pain and physical pain rely on a shared neural circuitry within similar brain regions.[173]

Other fMRI studies provide supporting evidence for the interaction between social pain and physical pain. Researchers found that physical pain and social pain rely on shared neural circuitry, suggesting that the experience of physical pain and social pain may have the same neurological basis. Ming Zhang et al. write: "Indeed, the neural activity in the 'pain matrix' is functionally heterogeneous, and part of it carries information related to pain fullness and intensity/salience. Negative experiences based on social pain can activate the brain regions related to the emotional components of physical pain, and psychological factors can influence pain perception." Over the years, neuroscientists have identified the pain matrix, a set of brain regions—including the anterior cingulate cortex, thalamus, and insula—that consistently responds to painful stimuli.

CHAPTER 10: PSYCHIC PAIN AND INTERSUBJECTIVITY

The Abandoned Child

The most severe form of child neglect is abandonment. In 1966, the communist dictator Nicolae Ceaușescu banned abortion and birth control in Romania to increase the country's birth rate. As a result, parents abandoned more than one hundred thousand children and left them at Romanian state institutions. Years later, the Romanian government tried to rectify the results of the policy, which had resulted in extreme child abuse and international disgrace. Romanian officials agreed to give investigators from the United States permission to conduct a comprehensive study of the detrimental effects of institutionalization on children's psychological and neurological development.

The randomized controlled study, which began in 2000 and was named the Bucharest Early Intervention Project (BEIP), looked at foster care as an intervention for children abandoned at or around the time of birth and placed in one of six institutions for young children in Bucharest, Romania. The first of its kind, the study compared a group of infants placed in foster care with another group raised in institutions, providing a level of experimental precision previously unavailable. It was the most scientific study ever done on the effects of institutional care on the neurological and emotional development of infants and young children. In a 2013 *Scientific American* article entitled "Anguish of the Abandoned Child," three distinguished professors— Charles Nelson III, Harvard Medical School; Nathan Fox, University of Maryland; and Charles Zeanah, Jr., Tulane University—wrote, "The plight of orphaned Romanian children reveals the psychic and physical scars from first years spent without a loving, responsive caregiver."[174]

Sensitive Periods

The main goal of the BEIP was to investigate the assumption that "early experience has a particularly strong influence in shaping the immature brain." The authors wrote the following regarding this most critical component of their research study:

The study set out to explore the premise that early experience often exerts a particularly strong influence in shaping the immature brain. For some behaviors, neural connections form in our early years in response to environmental influences during windows of time called sensitive periods. A child who listens to spoken language or simply looks around receives oral and visual inputs that shape neural connections during specific periods of development. The results of the study supported this initial premise of a sensitive period: the difference between an early life spent in an institution and one in foster care was dramatic. At thirty, forty, and fifty-two months, the average IQ of the institutionalized group was in the low to middle 70s, whereas it was about nineteen points higher for children in foster care. Not surprisingly, IQ was about 100, the standard range, for the group that had never been institutionalized. We also discovered a sensitive period when a child was able to achieve a maximum gain in IQ: a boy or girl placed in a home before roughly two years of age had a significantly higher IQ than one put there after that age.

The Romanian children living in institutions provide the best evidence to date that the initial two years of life constitute a sensitive period in which a child must receive intimate emotional and physical contact or else find personal development stymied. Infants learn from experience to seek comfort, support and protection from their significant caregivers, whether those individuals are natural or foster parents-and so we decided to measure attachment. Only extreme conditions that limit opportunities for a child to form attachments can interfere with a process that is a foundation for normal social development. When we measured this variable in the institutionalized children, we found that the overwhelming majority displayed incompletely formed and aberrant relationships with their caregivers.

When the children were forty-two months of age, we made another assessment and found that the children placed in foster care displayed dramatic improvements in making emotional attachments. Almost half had established secure relationships with another person whereas only eighteen percent of the institutionalized children had done so. Children placed into foster care before the end of the twenty-four-month sensitive period were more likely to form secure attachments compared with children placed there after that threshold.[175]

The authors provide real-life examples of how nurturing or denying positive attachment affects a child's development:

These numbers are more than just statistical disparities that separate the institutionalized and foster groups. They translate into very real experiences of both anguish and hope. Sebastian (none of the children's names in this article are real), now twelve, has spent virtually his entire life in an orphanage and has seen his IQ drop twenty points to a subpar sixty-four since he was tested during his fifth year. A youth who may have never formed an attachment with anyone, Sebastian drinks alcohol and displays other risk-prone behaviors. During an interview with us, he became irritable and interrupted with flashes of anger.

Bogdan, also twelve, illustrates the difference that receiving individualized attention from an adult makes. He was abandoned at birth and lived in the maternity ward until two months of age, after which he lived in an institution for nine months. He was then recruited into the project and randomized to the foster care group, where he was placed in the family of a single mother and her adolescent daughter. Bogdan started to catch up quickly and managed to overcome mild developmental delays within months. Although he had some behavioral problems, project staff members worked with the family, and by his fifth birthday the foster mother had decided to adopt him. At age twelve, Bogdan's IQ continues to score at an above-average level. He attends one of the best public schools in Bucharest and has the highest grades in his class.[176]

In addition to measuring IQ levels, the study used other variables related to emotional and physical health to compare and contrast the institutionalized children with those placed in a foster home. What follows is a short summary.

Language Development: The children who were raised in an institution had minimal adult interactions, and the lack of ongoing verbal communications with adults significantly impaired their language development. The children placed in foster care prior to about the age of fifteen or sixteen months showed normal language development.

CHAPTER 10: PSYCHIC PAIN AND INTERSUBJECTIVITY

Mental Health Problems: 53% of children who had lived in an institution received a psychiatric diagnosis by the age of four and a half, compared with 20% of those never institutionalized. Of note, 62% of the institutionalized children nearing the age of five received diagnoses ranging from anxiety disorders (44%) to attention-deficit/hyperactivity disorder (ADHD, 23%). The researchers concluded that foster care significantly reduced the level of anxiety and depression but didn't influence ADHD or conduct disorder. Moreover, they noted a direct correlation between a secure attachment with the foster parent and the remission of symptoms.

Brain Development: The researchers studied the effects on children's brain development of living in an institution versus a foster home. Measurement of brain activity revealed that infants living in institutions had significant reductions in one component of EEG activity and a heightened level in another. The conclusion was that such a pattern suggested delayed brain development. Those children were then reassessed at the eight-year mark. The researchers found that the electrical activity in the brains of children placed in foster care before two years of age was similar to that of children never institutionalized. Those children removed from an orphanage after two years and those who never left showed a less mature pattern of brain activity.

The authors write:

The noticeable decrease in EEG activity among the institutionalized children was perplexing. The institutionalized children showed a large reduction in the volume of both gray matter (neurons and other cells) and white matter (the insulating substance covering neurons' wirelike extensions).

In general, all the institutionalized children had smaller brain volumes. Placing children in foster care at any age had no effect on increasing the amount of gray matter—the foster care group showed levels of gray matter comparable to those of the institutionalized children. However, the foster care children showed more white matter volume than the institutionalized group.[177]

Neuroimaging Study of Neural Correlates of Social Exclusion

In what is now seen as a pioneering neuroimaging study, Naomi Eisenberger et al. tested the hypothesis that the brain experiences social pain in a similar way to physical pain. The authors wrote:

It is a basic feature of human experience to feel soothed in the presence of close others and to feel distressed when left behind. Many languages reflect this experience in the assignment of physical pain words ("hurt feelings") to describe experiences of social separation. However, the notion that the pain associated with losing someone is similar to the pain experienced upon physical injury seems more metaphorical than real. Nonetheless, evidence suggests that some of the same neural machinery recruited in the experience of physical pain may also be involved in the experience of pain associated with social separation or rejection. Because of the adaptive value of mammalian social bonds, the social attachment system, which keeps young near caregivers, may have piggybacked onto the physical pain system to promote

CHAPTER 10: PSYCHIC PAIN AND INTERSUBJECTIVITY

survival. We conducted a functional magnetic resonance imaging (fMRI) study of social exclusion to determine whether the regions activated by social pain are similar to those found in studies of physical pain.

The anterior cingulate cortex (ACC) is believed to act as a neural "alarm system" or conflict monitor, detecting when an automatic response is inappropriate or in conflict with current goals Not surprisingly, pain, the most primitive signal that "something is wrong," activates the ACC. More specifically, dorsal ACC activity is primarily associated with the affectively distressing rather than the sensory component of pain.

Because of the importance of social bonds for the survival of most mammalian species, the social attachment system may have adopted the neural computations of the ACC, involved in pain and conflict detection processes, to promote the goal of social connectedness.[178]

Eisenberger's study suggests that social pain is analogous to physical pain in its neurocognitive function: it alerts us when we have sustained injury to our social connections and allows restorative measures to be taken. Understanding the underlying commonalities between physical and social pain helps us grasp why physical and social pain are affected similarly by social support and neurochemical interventions and why it "hurts" to lose someone we love.

It's not unusual for residents of a treatment center to bolt from the facility. As mentioned in chapter 6, whenever I asked such patients why they had run away, they invariably gave the same answer: they had been trying to return home to be with their mother. Individuals who have been rejected by or separated from their birth mother suffer lifelong psychological pain. Many patients, children and adults alike, would tell me that they would rather suffer physical abuse by their parents than be rejected, abandoned, and physically and emotionally separated from their biological parents, especially their mother.

Regardless of the pain suffered, children, in order to be whole, continue to try to win their mother's love so they can feel a sense of truly being wanted. I treated many children, adolescents, and adults who had been physically abused and severely neglected. As mentioned in chapter 1, most told me they would rather have been beaten with a belt than rejected by their mother. In the words of Martin Buber, "All pain (psychic) is intersubjective as we are in pain because of someone else."

Main Conclusions of the Bucharest Early Intervention Project

Early childhood experiences have a profound impact on brain development.

Foster care does not remediate the serious developmental abnormalities associated with being raised in an institution. It does, however, enable a child to develop in a healthier way.

During sensitive periods, recovery from deprivation occurs as soon as a child begins to experience a more favorable living environment (this is perhaps the study's biggest takeaway).

The sooner children are cared for by stable, emotionally invested caregivers, the more likely they are to follow a more normal developmental trajectory.

Psychological Evaluation of an Abandoned and Rejected Child

Years ago, I assessed Tamika, a sixteen-year-old girl who had been abandoned at a young age. Below is a synopsis of her comprehensive psychological evaluation. Her case material illustrates the devastating real-life effects of early abandonment, neglect, abuse, and toxic environmental stress on long-term adolescent psychological functioning.

Reason for Referral

The court ordered Tamika to submit to a psychological evaluation as a resident of the juvenile center. Her child services case worker wanted to rule out schizophrenia and bipolar disorder because her family had a history of such disorders. Tamika also participated in cognitive and personality testing.

Clinical Interview

Tamika initially offered limited information and was uncooperative during our interview. She attempted to leave my office twice. I had no problem, however, in redirecting her to complete the interview. Tamika presented with minimal concerns during testing. She would respond to my questions while hunched over her knees or while resting her head on the table, all the while complaining that the lights were too bright. Or she would sit on her chair with her back to me and would tilt her head back and stare up at the ceiling. She was alert and cooperative during my assessments and revealed a sense of energy and spontaneity. She even sang during the interview process. She made limited eye contact with me and became guarded when she was asked about specific topics. "No comment," she would respond.

Tamika was born in Chicago. At the age of five, she was removed from her parents' custody due to domestic abuse and neglect.

"What was it like growing up?" I asked.

She shrugged. "It was chaotic growing up in my house. They were always fighting."

"*Who* was fighting?"

"My parents. They were always fighting about everything. They used to get physical with each other. I saw them shoot each other. My dad pulled out a gun and accidentally shot himself in the ankle and then shot my mom in the knee. Then I was removed from my parents for domestic abuse and neglect. I lived all over the area. I was in foster care at five years old. I was with my siblings during the first home. We only lasted two days before we were separated."

"Tell me about your mother," I said.

She bristled. "No comment. I'm not going to say anything that will get her in trouble. I know how you people do things."

I continued to press, and Tamika eventually described her relationship with her mother as good.

"What about your father?"

"My dad has been in jail for a year for having possession of a gun. I guess I used to like him."

Tamika was the third oldest of ten children in a blended family. Seven children were from her mother's side, and her father had another three boys who lived with their mother. Tamika reported having a good relationship with her older siblings.

CHAPTER 10: PSYCHIC PAIN AND INTERSUBJECTIVITY

"Can you tell me about some of your traumatic experiences as a child?" I asked.

She stared up at the ceiling. "My dad would always hit us."

"That sounds awful. How did you cope?"

"I thought it was normal and thought all parents did that." She shrugged again.

"Were you ever sexually abused?"

Her eyes narrowed in anger and distrust. "No comment. I've already told people what happened, and no one believes me, so why would you? So no comment."

Tamika was in the eleventh grade and told me she had received all As and one C+ on her last report card. She revealed that her favorite class was music and that she enjoyed karaoke day. Her least favorite place at school was the resource room.

"How do you get along with your teachers and other students?"

"I have great relationships with my teachers."

Tamika had never been enrolled in special education classes, but she had an IEP (individualized education program) in place due to behavioral concerns and her diagnosis of ADHD.

"Have you ever been suspended or expelled from school?"

"I got expelled for trying to beat up my principal," she said matter-of-factly, "and I was suspended several times in middle school for fighting. I almost got expelled for fighting a girl."

"What are your future goals?"

Tamika's face didn't exactly light up, but she revealed a hint of enthusiasm in her answer. "My goal is to be a mental health technician. My dream is for me and my brothers to spend lots of time together. In five years, I'll be able to be with my brothers.

We can do sibling things. One will be twenty-one, and the other will be eighteen, so he can get out of the system, and we can all be together."

I thought for a moment. "Tell me about an average day. What do you do?"

"I laugh the whole day. But I also listen to hip hop." She paused a moment. "I like singing and watching TV shows."

"Do you have any friends?"

"Friends? What friends? I got myself."

It wasn't the first time I'd listened as a troubled teen tried to pretend she was stronger than she was, but my heart ached for Tamika nonetheless. "Have you ever been bullied in school?"

Her defiant nature returned. "No comment. I won't answer that."

"Do you have a boyfriend?"

"Yeah. We've been together four years."

"Are you two sexually active?"

She nodded.

"Are you affiliated with any gangs?"

"Hmm." She smiled. "I don't know what you're talking about."

I decided to return to the topic of her family. "Does your family have a history of drug or alcohol use?"

"Yeah." She nodded. "My mom and dad did something."

"What type of drugs did they use?"

"I don't know what was allowed or around when they were using. My dad's in jail now, so he's not using it."

"What about you? Do you use drugs?"

She shook her head. "No, I don't do anything."

CHAPTER 10: PSYCHIC PAIN AND INTERSUBJECTIVITY

When I asked Tamika about any medical or psychological disorders that might run in her family, she said she wasn't aware of any. For her part, she said she had been diagnosed with depression, borderline personality disorder, and ADHD. She was currently taking Prozac, Seroquel, and Trazadone.

"What about therapy?"

"Well, I get it once a week, on Wednesdays, and I just don't care for it. It kind of works."

As we dug deeper, Tamika told me that she wasn't interested in future counseling. She said she hadn't perceived any changes to her sleeping patterns or appetite. Nor had she entertained an increase in thoughts of sadness.

"Have you ever tried to harm yourself?"

She nodded. "I tried to hang myself two weeks ago at the previous detention center and was found unconscious."

"What caused you to entertain thoughts of suicide?"

"I don't know." Another shrug. "I just wanted to die." She paused a beat. "It wasn't the first time I've tried."

I quizzed her about her previous attempts, but she refused to talk about them.

"Generally speaking," I said, "how would you describe yourself?"

"I'm an active person."

"What do you think you need to work on most in your life right now?"

She appeared to think for a moment. "Accepting no. And that's it."

Cognitive Evaluation

I assessed Tamika's full-scale intellectual functioning to be in the average range. There is a ninety-five percent level of confidence that her actual or "true" score fell between eighty-seven and ninety-eight.

Personality Evaluation

Tamika identified "body/looks" and "weight/eating issues" as the problems that were troubling her the most. Her emotional needs for affection, nurturance, and safety were central to her personality makeup, and her needs were highly associated with her diminished level of psychological functioning and were directly correlated with her psychopathology. She maintained low self-esteem and self-reported perceptions of physical and social inadequacy. She was submissive and dependent. She tended to subjugate her own needs to the expectations of others to gain their acceptance. Her fear of abandonment caused her to behave in an affable, compliant manner to gain the nurturance and emotional support she desired.

Tamika lacked a clear sense of self or identity. She had experienced a considerable degree of psychological pain throughout her formative years and every day since. She didn't appear to have formed close emotional attachments throughout her life and thus related to others in a superficial manner in order to avoid the pain of further rejection. She viewed herself as a "victim," but while doing so, she disowned and rationalized her impulsivity and negative and irresponsible behaviors. She was highly conflicted and vacillated between internalizing her feelings and externalizing them, and she struggled to maintain

CHAPTER 10: PSYCHIC PAIN AND INTERSUBJECTIVITY

a consistent state of psychological equilibrium. Sometimes, she behaved in an intropunitive way through withdrawal or self-destructive acts. At other times, she engaged in oppositional defiance or aberrant behavior. Her limited capacity to modulate her moods was a primary characteristic of her personality.

Tamika's self-deprecating, flat, depressive affect, lack of social initiative, diminished energy, internal numbness, and dissociative thinking signified her state of anhedonia (inability to experience pleasure or joy). Likewise, her personality was characterized by alexithymia: a state of deficiency in understanding, processing, or describing emotions. Tamika was "cut off" from her own internal functioning and seemed void of a sense of self or identity. Her internal detachment suggested a sense of depersonalization, which spoke to her lack of self-awareness and her sense of detachment from herself. Her sense of existence and fragmented self-image was the antithesis of a fully functioning, well-integrated, egosyntonic individual, and her depersonalization was a core component of her personality. The chronic nature of her depersonalization was associated with the effects of traumatic life events.

There was a core component of depression inherent in Tamika's personality. She lacked a sense of energy and spontaneity and was rather lethargic. She feared engaging in emotionally intimate, interpersonal relationships, and she feared that disclosing her feelings and problems would render her vulnerable to others. Along with interacting with others in a superficial manner, she feared criticism and rejection. She had internalized her emptiness, loneliness, depression, and extreme emotional pain.

Tamika's personality also showed avoidant, schizotypal, and borderline features, which, in conjunction with her previously discussed personality characteristics, exacerbated her poor psychological functioning. Her ability to engage in human interaction was grossly impaired. It was as if Tamika was socially handicapped. She was unable to attain fulfillment of her needs for affection, nurturance, acceptance, and security, and she was internally conflicted because she avoided, mistrusted, and feared that which she so desperately sought: human contact, validation, dependency, and emotional intimacy. It was likely that her currently assessed borderline personality features and depression were due to physical and sexual abuse, parental abandonment, toxic environmental stress, and countless foster home placements.

Tamika possessed many of the differentiating characteristics associated with borderline personality features, including the following:

- Somewhat disordered, quasi-psychotic thinking
- Self-destructive behaviors
- Suicidal ideations
- Abandonment issues
- Demanding behavior
- Treatment regressions
- Absence of boundaries

There are usually three primary comorbid features associated with the above-noted borderline characteristics:

CHAPTER 10: PSYCHIC PAIN AND INTERSUBJECTIVITY

- A developmental history of insecure attachment and poor adjustment
- Inadequate or hostile parental care
- Stressful or chaotic life circumstances

A quality of dysphoric mood pervaded Tamika's daily life. She became self-destructive with her pent-up emotions. She would need to develop a better "locus of control" or internalized superego to balance and regulate her strong, conflicting, oppositional-defiant impulses and emotions. She would need to become more egosyntonic—i.e., her overall psychological functioning, including her behaviors, values, and feelings that were in harmony with her own needs and self-image, would need to become more internalized. To accomplish this, she would need to actively treat and remediate her mood swings, alter her dysfunctional behavioral patterns, and improve her self-esteem.

I didn't assess Tamika to be purposefully malicious or hostile. Rather, she was in a considerable degree of emotional pain and craved affection and nurturance. She lacked the internal psychological resources, self-esteem, and socialization skills with which to effectively engage peers and adults. More recently, she had been "acting out" or externalizing her pent-up dysphoric mood and anger. For the most part, however, she was prone to engage in self-destructive thoughts or actions. Her self-hatred permeated her thoughts and significantly impaired her overall level of psychological functioning. She was preoccupied with her body image, which speaks to the severe level of her anxiety, sadness, and pain.

I recommended that Tamika be referred to a residential treatment center. It was my opinion that she required a more highly structured and therapeutically intensive setting to treat the problems noted in my evaluation. She lacked psychological resources, confidence, energy, self-esteem, and judgment. Her overall level of psychological functioning was significantly impaired.

It was my opinion that Tamika's assessed Persistent Depressive, Posttraumatic Stress, and Reactive Attachment Disorders placed her at risk for continued norm violations at home, at school, and in the community. Her problems were pervasive and highly self-destructive in nature, which made her a potential danger to herself and others.

CHAPTER 11

Hands-on Parenting

"Actions speak louder than words; let your words teach and your actions speak."
— St. Anthony of Padua, circa 1222

We need a license to drive, a permit to remodel our home, and a passport to travel abroad, but anyone can be a parent. As prospective parents, we might take classes or read a book or two on parenting before our child is born, but far too many of us parent by the seat of our pants. We remember how we were raised and, depending on how we view our upbringing, emulate or ignore our parents' methods. Our children are born without instruction manuals, and no matter how much research we do before they arrive, nothing can prepare us for the deep sense of responsibility—not to mention the utter exhaustion and confusion—we experience once we've left the hospital and embark on our parenting journey. Family, friends, and neighbors might offer assistance, but ultimately we're responsible for our children and how they're raised.

In this chapter, we move from the theoretical to the practical. What does it mean to be a responsive, sensitive parent? Rather than present a nuts-and-bolts guide to parenting, I'm going to help orient you. If the preceding chapters were all about the science of parenting, this one is dedicated to the art. Put another way, although the science clearly points to responsive, sensitive parenting as *best-practice* parenting, it doesn't confine us to a set of techniques or dictums. Rather, it opens our minds to a whole new way of looking at parenting. In this chapter, I'm not going to tell you how often to change your child's diaper or when to have "the talk" about the birds and the bees. Instead, I'm going to give you a lens through which to view every parenting choice you make. If you cleave to the following approach, you'll give your child their best chance to grow into a healthy adult.

Responsive, sensitive parenting is hands-on parenting. It requires that you possess two things in abundance: time and energy. Without both, you won't be able to meet your child's needs. Indeed, parenting is the biggest commitment you'll ever make precisely because it demands so much of you. But as challenging as it is, parenting ultimately serves as the most rewarding endeavor you'll ever undertake. Much is required, and much is given in return.

Responsive, sensitive parenting doesn't look the same for everyone, because no parent-child relationship is the same. But it requires the same general orientation, no matter the specifics at play. Below we'll explore the four pillars of our approach. Responsive, sensitive parenting is (1) relational, (2) accepting, (3) energetic, and (4) attuned. Let's take a closer look.

CHAPTER 11: HANDS-ON PARENTING

The Relational Mindset

Responsive, sensitive parenting is relational. It requires an ongoing interactive, collaborative process. It involves emotional interactions that play out continually, day after day. To be your best during those interactions, practice serve and return:

1. Notice the serve and share the child's focus of attention.
2. Return the serve.
3. Be supporting and encouraging.
4. Give it a name!
5. Take turns... and wait. Keep the interaction going back and forth.
6. Practice endings and beginnings.

Your relationship with your child is bilateral, collaborative, and intersubjective. You are your child's first companion, and you grow as your child grows. On a deeper level, your relationship with your child constitutes their first and most important I-Thou relationship. Nurture and protect it as the sacred relationship that it is!

The Accepting Mindset

Responsive, sensitive parenting requires your acceptance. You must not only accept your child as unique and the owner of a unique mind; you must give your child unconditional positive regard, even when you disapprove of or feel disappointed by your child's actions. As a parent, you are your child's first and most important attachment. As such, you can offer no greater gift than recognition and acceptance of your child's unique identity, which is singular, whole, and separate from yours.

The Energetic Mindset

Responsive, sensitive parenting requires your energy and exertion. Along with making yourself physically and emotionally available, you must practice patience as your child develops naturally and at a pace unique to them. Giving your energy means communicating openly, which you can begin when your child is a newborn by engaging in protoconversation. It means offering compassion and empathy—even and especially when you don't feel like it. It means fulfilling the role of expert and exerting your imagination. It means holding and touching your child, playing with your child, and encouraging your child to self-play.

It means stimulating your child:

1. Verbal stimulation increases your child's social-emotional development.
2. Extracurricular activities increase self-confidence, social skills (prosocial and empathy), new skills, friendships, self-integration, responsibility, and enrichment.
3. Reading aloud to your child facilitates literacy and stimulates brain, social, and emotional development.
4. Reading proficiency by third grade is the most significant predictor of high school graduation and career success.

It means practicing the four core elements of dialogue: turning, addressing, listening, and responding.

1. *Turning:* Reorienting your focus from yourself to your child
2. *Addressing:* Willingly and unconditionally accepting your

child as a unique person who is capable and permitted to voice their own ideas
3. *Listening:* Being empathic and understanding your child's own frame of reference—how he or she sees the world
4. *Responding:* Responding in an honest, kind, and sensitive manner

The Attuned Mindset

Responsive, sensitive parenting requires you to tune in to your child's needs. Doing so takes practice but eventually becomes intuitive. If you pay attention, and if you see your child as a unique individual with unique needs and a unique perspective, you'll begin to notice your child's cues. Once you understand those cues and what they mean, you'll know how best to respond to them. Indeed, you'll become a mindreader of sorts, ever in tune with your child's feelings and needs.

A newborn innately expects emotional responsiveness and satiation of their affect hunger at birth. Similarly, a mother's brain and physiology is biochemically ready to provide emotional responsiveness and provisions of warmth, nurturance, and safety. By maintaining an attuned mindset, we're making good on our biological programming. Even if parenting doesn't come naturally to us, we can use what we know about nature's coding to best meet our child's needs.

Maintaining an attuned mindset requires that we practice "mind-mindedness," which can be summarized as follows:

1. Treat your newborn and infant not merely as an entity to be satisfied but as someone who has a mind of their own.

2. Tune in to what your infant or child might be thinking or feeling.
3. Learn to know your child's cues and unique features.
4. Be sensitive to and aware of your child's cues and strive to accurately interpret them.
5. Respond promptly and appropriately to your child's cues.
6. Be selectively and sensitively attuned to your child's internal states and unique thoughts, feelings, and frame of reference.

If you consistently maintain the four mindsets explored above—relational, accepting, energetic, attuned—you will become a responsive, sensitive parent. You won't be perfect. You'll still make mistakes. But you'll be engaging in best-practice parenting that reflects the most up-to-date scientific consensus.

CHAPTER 12

Conclusions

"Whoever saves a single soul, it is as if they saved an entire world."
— JERUSALEM TALMUD SANHEDRIN 4:9:1

TODAY WE POSSESS the scientific knowledge to help parents and caregivers "know better and do better." Major breakthroughs in neuroscience and the integration of these revolutionary findings with theoretical psychological formulations give us a comprehensive understanding of the newborn infant. Previous long-held beliefs have been discarded, and the account of the human infant's development based on philosophy and medical and psychological sciences has been rewritten. A newborn has innate mental capacities. Shortly after birth, infants reveal cultural intelligence and the motivation of innate intersubjective sympathy. We are born to generate shifting states of self-awareness, to show them to other people, and to provoke interest and affectionate responses.

This new developmental and functional neuroscience of the human brain contradicts former experts who claimed infants knew nothing and were incapable of acting. The philosopher René Descartes theorized that the individual self is all that can be known to exist. Such solipsism and belief that "only my mind exists" has been replaced with the "self born in intersubjectivity." Sigmund Freud and Jean Piaget, who posited that a newborn was a *tabula rasa* or empty slate, likewise have been proven wrong. And the primary viewpoint of behaviorists who focus on externally observed actions has been supplanted by theory of mind and intersubjectivity. Such a psychological perspective of the newborn's innate potential for early social and emotional awareness, human communication, and interaction reveals the opportunity to significantly enrich your child's psychological development, beginning at birth.

In this book, I've presented three central concepts: affect hunger; responsive, sensitive parenting; and intersubjectivity. And I've discussed four key psychological resources or personality components, all of which are interrelated. If you practice, provide, and internalize them, your child will likely achieve healthy psychological development. The material in the prior chapters forms a synthesis of scientific findings with my own evidence-based clinical practice data, findings, and experience. I've approached each topic from a holistic or biopsychosocial perspective. The boundaries and discussion of child development are increasingly porous. In fact, many of the advancements in child development and parenting are the result of increased sharing and understanding of the interactive effects of psychological and neuroscientific factors. The painstaking, lifelong work of many research pioneers in neuroscience and psychology over the past fifty years has resulted in our radically different understanding of the infant. The central, indispensable concept underlying the subject matter discussed within each previous chapter is intersubjectivity. It's the primary feature inherent in healthy psychological development.

Let's briefly summarize the key points in the core chapters.

Affect Hunger: Affect hunger is an emotional hunger for maternal love and those other feelings of protection and care implied in the mother-child relationship. The infant possesses an innate need to experience feelings or emotions at birth, and this need motivates all infants and children to connect with their birth mother. Such a drive originates in the most primitive part of the mammalian brain. A newborn expects immediate reception of affect and emotional responsiveness. The neglect of such emotional responsiveness and maternal attachment disturbs the infant's homeostasis and affects brain functioning.

A child's maternal attachment is critical in parenting. Successful emotional bonding significantly increases the chances of normal psychological development. If the mother-child bond is disrupted in the early stages, there exists a high risk for emotional problems, poor social adjustment, psychological disorders, underachievement, learning disorders, and impaired brain architecture.

The core attribute associated with affect hunger, touch is the infant's primary craving for both survival and comfort. Tactile stimulation is the infant's first language. The qualitative and quantitative nature of that felt communication represents the primary source of warmth, safety, nurturance, and love for the infant.

Conscience: The most severe characterological deficit is the lack of an ingrained conscience—that inner voice and intuitive sense that gauges the morality of our behavior and serves as an indication that we've successfully adapted to the rules and norms of our culture. A conscience means that we can function in the world as a responsible citizen. Without a moral compass, we are flawed, less human, and a danger to ourselves and others.

Empathy: The ability to understand another person's thoughts and feelings from their point of view, rather than our own, constitutes empathy. If we have empathy, we have the ability to sensitively and accurately—but not sympathetically—understand our child's experience and feelings in the here-and-now.

Play: When children are asked what they like to do more than anything else, the most common answer is to play, which brings them great joy. We now know that the brain contains distinct neural systems devoted to roughhousing or rough-and-tumble (RAT) play. An essential component of healthy child development, play is synonymous with learning and creativity. A child's capacity to play imaginatively is directly linked to their level of psychological well-being.

Stimulation: Evidence-based research emphasizes two primary forms of parent-child stimulation: verbal communication and social interaction. In my clinical work, I observed another critical type of stimulation: extracurricular activities.

CHAPTER 12: CONCLUSIONS

Without it, children experience boredom, malaise, and poor social skills.

Findings conclude that maternal and paternal sensitivity and verbal stimulation predict increases in a child's social-emotional development. Parental stimulation is essential for your child's social and emotional development, not to mention optimal brain development.

Responsive, Sensitive Parenting: John Bowlby, if you'll recall, noted in his formulation of attachment theory that responsive, sensitive parenting refers to family interactions in which parents are aware of their child's emotional and physical needs and respond appropriately and consistently. Sensitive parents are in tune with their children. Successful parenting means respecting your child as a unique individual with a mind of their own. As the best-practice model for responding to your child's innate intersubjective motives and capabilities, responsive, sensitive parenting serves as the surest way to provide your child with the social and emotional stimulation and back-and-forth interactions he or she needs.

Securely attached mothers are more attuned to their babies than mothers who are insecurely attached. Secure mothers attune to a range of infant affect, whereas insecure mothers tend not to attune to negative affect. Children who receive responsive, sensitive care from their parents form more secure attachment relationships and possess a greater capacity to manage stress. Such an attachment is critical in the child's development of resilience.

Psychology and Intersubjectivity: Carl Rogers proposed that three characteristics form the core components of a parent's relationship with their child: congruence, unconditional positive regard (UPR), and accurate empathic understanding. Martin Buber emphasized that the essence of being human is to engage in genuine meeting, conversation, or dialogue through social relationships. Successful parenting requires that we enter into a genuine, collaborative, respectful I-Thou relationship with our children.

Affective Neuroscience: In early pregnancy, an embryo's brain creates 250,000 new neurons per minute. Recent evidence from neuroscience shows that babies have as many neurons as adults and that stimulation is necessary to form connections between them for growth and learning. This means babies are equipped to learn through their multisensory experiences. Early on, infants can perceive and respond to another's affective state. Infants come to experience emotions as shared states and learn to differentiate their own states partly by witnessing the responses that they elicit in others.

The discovery of the mirror neuron system provides clear scientific evidence that intersubjective experiences are mapped onto an individual's cerebral functioning from the first years of life. Vittorio Gallese's extensive research on the mirror neuron system provides the neurological explanation that links the infant/parent responsivity to the brain within the maternal empathy and mirror neuron theory. The mirror neurons are a special category of brain cells that fire simultaneously when a person performs a motor action and an observer or "other" witnesses them making the same movement. Such a finding has dramatically altered our understanding of the human as a social animal within the context of an intersubjective connection and alterity of the other.

Overall, psychobiological studies are revealing that mother-infant systems are intercorrelated within a superordinate organization that allows mutual regulation of cerebral, biochemical, and autonomic processes. Through these "hidden" mechanisms, the adult brain works as an external regulatory and organizing system that favors the development of the infant's immature homeostatic functioning. In such a context, attachment is not just an overt behavior; it's an internal organization built into the nervous system in the course and as a result of the infant's experience of their transactions with the mother.

Neurological findings indicate maternal transformations of the mother's brain during pregnancy. Structural changes occur, including the size of some neurons, which increase the mother's ability to decode her infant's emotional expressions and respond in a more highly attuned, sensitive way. This concept of embodiment is used to explain how neurobiological events are sought to account for mental events. By means of "embodied simulation," internal representations of the body states associated with actions, emotions, and sensations are evoked in the observer, as in the case of mothers, as though they would be doing a similar action or experiencing a similar emotion or sensation. In this way, the Mirror Neurons System (MNS) can be described as the neurobiological correlate of intersubjective system, since it represents the innate and embodied motivation to be in contact with others' emotions and to share subjective experiences with them.

Psychic Pain: Throughout my years of practice, I found a high correlation between psychic pain and affect hunger. Such a co-occurrence is diagnostic and suggests insufficient responsive care during the formative years of development. It points to the neglect of innate neurochemical, biological, and psychological needs for maternal and paternal affection and interactions.

Powerfully inducing feelings of social rejection activates regions of the brain that are involved in physical pain sensation—rarely activated in neuroimaging studies of emotion. Such findings are consistent with the idea that the experience of social rejection—or social loss, more generally—may represent a distinct emotional experience that is uniquely associated with physical pain.

A handful of functional magnetic resonance imaging (fMRI) studies provide supporting evidence for the interaction between social pain and physical pain. It was found that physical pain and social pain rely on shared neural circuitry, suggesting that the experience of physical pain and social pain may have the same neurological basis. The pioneering study by Naomi Eisenberger et al. explored in chapter 10, meanwhile, showed that the brain alerts us when we have sustained an injury to our social connections and prompts us to take restorative measures.

Bucharest Early Intervention Project (BEIP): In chapter 10, we explored the findings of the BEIP, which studied the plight of Romanian orphans. Researchers concluded that newborns, infants, and young children who grow up without a loving, responsive caregiver bear lasting psychic and physical

CHAPTER 12: CONCLUSIONS

scars. Foster care can't remediate the immediate results of such neglect, but the earlier we intervene in children's care, the better chance they have to grow into healthy adults. During sensitive periods, recovery from deprivation occurs as soon as a child begins to experience a more favorable living environment (this is perhaps the study's biggest takeaway).

༄

I've provided essential components to help you better parent your child and maximize their potential for healthy social, emotional, and cognitive development. You now have the skillset and guidelines. Such parenting takes daily practice. The more you relate to your child as a unique person with a mind of their own, the more you read their cues, the better you will understand their inner emotional world. Doing so will increase your sensitivity to your child and your ability to selectively attune and respond to their immediate and ever-changing needs. You will become an expert in reading your child's cues and inner thoughts and feelings.

A child who has received responsive, sensitive parenting, whose hunger for affect has been well satiated, is likely to grow into a healthy adult. We humans require a long period of gestation. By practicing the parenting and skills discussed in this book, you give your child the potential to thrive.

After five decades of treating and formally evaluating children, adolescents, and adults, I've come to identify a set of personality features associated with thriving people. Such individuals have energy and are empathic, compassionate, emotionally spontaneous, self-revealing, and generous. They've individuated—that is, they're self-reliant, responsible, motivated, and compassionate to others. They possess a sense of meaning and purpose in their lives and a feeling of wholeness or congruency, and they easily engage in genuine dialogue and emotionally intimate I-Thou relationships. They're actively involved in their communities and show concern for the common good and welfare of others. They have significantly achieved their innate potential for healthy social, emotional, and cognitive functioning.

Our mission is singular in nature: to enable our child to function independently. This means acquiring all the necessary emotional and psychological nutrients to seek out their own special place in the world, free from most parental signals. It means enabling our children to outlast us. Our children must do more than exist; they must find fulfillment. They must do more than survive; they must thrive.

In *Superman*, Jor-El speaks with his son Kal-El before the young boy is transported to Earth:

> *You will travel far, my little Kal-El, but we will never leave you—even in the face of our deaths. You will make my strength your own. You will see my life through your eyes, as your life will be seen through mine. The son becomes the father, and the father, the son.*

ENDNOTES

1. Beck, S.J. *Rorschach's Test*. New York: Grune & Stratton, 1945.
2. Levy, D.M., *Maternal Overprotection*. New York: Columbia University Press, 1943.
3. Levy, D.M., "Finger sucking and accessory movements in infancy." *American Journal of Psychiatry*, 7:881, 1928.; Levy, D.M., & Beck, S.J., "The Rorschach test in manic-depressive psychosis." *American Journal of Orthopsychiatry*, 4:31-32, 1934.
4. Harlow, H.F., "The nature of love." *Amer. Psychol.* 13:673-695, 1958; Harlow, H.F. "Love in infant monkeys." *Scientific American*, June 1959.
5. Levy, D.M., "Primary Affect Hunger," American Journal of Psychiatry 94 (November 1937): 643-52.
6. APA, 2022.
7. Sroufe, L.A., Egeland, B., Carlson, E.A., & Collins, W.A. *The Development of the Person: The Minnesota Study of Risk and Adaptation from Birth to Adulthood*. New York: The Guilford Press, 2005.
8. Harlow, H.F. & Zimmermann, R.R. "The development of affective responsiveness in infant monkeys." *Proceedings of the American Philosophical Society*, 102:501-509.88, 1958.
9. Bowlby, J. *Attachment and loss: Vol. 1. Loss*. New York: Basic Books, 1969.
10. Schaffer, H.R., & Emerson, P.E. *The development of social attachments in infancy*. Monographs of the Society for Research in Child Development, 1-77, 1964.
11. Rutter, M. *Maternal deprivation reassessed*. Penguin Education: Harmondsworth, 1972.
12. Rutter, M. "Maternal deprivation, 1971-1978: new findings, new concepts, new approaches." *Child Development*, 50(2):283-305, 1979.
13. Hopper, H.E., & Pinneau, S.R. "Frequency of regurgitation in infancy as related to the amount of stimulation received from the mother." *Child Development*, 28, 229-235, 1957.
14. Liu, D., Diorio, J., Day, J.C., Francis, D.D., & Meaney, M.J. "Maternal care, hippocampal synaptogenesis and cognitive development

in rats." *Nature Neuroscience* 2000, Aug;3(8): 799-806. DOI: 10.1038/77702.

15 Rose, J.K., Sangha, S., Rai, S., Norman, K.R., & Rankin, C.H. "Decreased Sensory Stimulation Reduces Behavioral Responding, Retards Development, and Alters Neuronal Connectivity in Caenorhabditis elegans." *Journal of Neuroscience* 3, August 2005, 25 (31):7159-7168; DOI: https://doi.org/10.1523/JNEUROSCI.1833-05.2005.

16 Cady, S.H., & Jones, G.E. "Massage therapy as a workplace intervention for reduction of stress." *Perceptual & Motor Skills* 84, 157-158, 1997.

17 Field, T., Peck, M., Krugman, S., Tuchel, T., Schanberg, S., Kuhn, C., & Burman, I. "Burn injuries benefit from massage therapy." *J Burn Care Rehabilitation* 1998 May-Jun;19(3):241-4. DOI: 10.1097/00004630-199805000-00010. PMID: 9622469.

18 Diego, M.A., Field, T., Hernandez-Reif, M., Shaw, K., Friedman, L., Ironson, G. "HIV Adolescents Show Improved Immune Function Following Massage Therapy." *International Journal of Neuroscience* 106:1-2, 35-45, 2001. DOI:10.3109/00207450109149736

19 APA: Online Dictionary of Psychology.

20 Harvard University Center on the Developing Child, 2013.

21 Thompson, R.A., & Winer, A.C. "Moral development, conversation, and the development of internal working models." In C. Wainryb & H.E. Recchia, eds., *Talking about right and wrong: Parent-child conversations as contexts for moral development*. Cambridge: Cambridge University Press, 2014.

22 Kochanska, G., Koenig, J.L., Barry, R.A., Kim, S., & Yoon, J.E. "Children's conscience during toddler and preschool years, moral self, and a competent, adaptive developmental trajectory." *Developmental Psychology*, 46(5):1320, 2010.

23 de Rosnay, M., & Fink, E. "The development of moral motivation at 6 years of age." In R. Langdon & C. Mackenzie, eds., *Emotions, Imagination, and Moral Reasoning*. New York: Psychology Press, 2012.

24 Brenner, A. "Internalization, Internal Conflict, and I–Thou Relationships." *Philosophy, Psychiatry, and Psychology* 21(1):67-70, 2014.

25 Fox, N.A. "The Development of Emotion Regulation. Biological and

Behavioral Considerations." *Monographs of the Society for Research in Child Development* 59, 1994.

26 Bell, M.A., & Wolfe, C.D. "The cognitive neuroscience of early socioemotional development." In: C.A. Brownell & C.B. Kopp, eds., *Socioemotional Development in Toddler Years*. New York: Guilford Press, 2007.

27 Eisenberg, N., & Eggum, N.D. "Empathic responding: sympathy and personal distress." In: J. Decety & W. Ickes, eds., *The Social Neuroscience of Empathy*. Cambridge: MIT Press, 2009.

28 Bloom, P. "The Moral Life of Babies." *The New York Times Magazine*, May 5, 2010.

29 Rogers, C.R.; Dorfman, E., Gordon, T. & Hobbs, N. (contributors). *Client-Centered Therapy. Its Current Practice, Implications, and Theory*. Boston: Houghton Mifflin Company, 1951.

30 Kim, S., & Kochanska, G. "Relational antecedents and social implications of the emotion of empathy: Evidence from three studies." *Emotion*, 17(6):981–992, 2017. DOI: https://doi.org/10.1037/emo0000297

31 Stern, J.A., Borelli, J.L., & Smiley, P.A. "Assessing parental empathy: A role for empathy in child attachment." *Attachment & Human Development*, 17(1):1–22, 2014. DOI: https://doi.org/10.1080/14616734.2014.969749

32 Bowlby, 1969.

33 Ainsworth, M.D.S. *Infancy in Uganda*. Baltimore: Johns Hopkins University Press, 1967; Ainsworth, M.D. "Attachment and dependency: A comparison." In J. L. Gewirtz, ed., *Attachment and dependency*. Washington, D.C.: V. H. Winston & Sons, 1972.

34 Stern et al., 2014.

35 Benita, M., Levkovitz, T., & Roth, G. "Integrative emotion regulation predicts adolescents' prosocial behavior through the mediation of empathy." *Learning and Instruction*, 50:14–20, 2017. DOI: https://doi.org/10.1016/j.learninstruc.2016.11.004

36 Miller, P.A., & Eisenberg, N. "The relation of empathy to aggressive and externalizing/antisocial behavior." *Psychological Bulletin*, 103(3):324–344, 1988. DOI: https://doi.org/10.1037/0033-2909.103.3.324

37 Decety, J. "The Neurodevelopment of Empathy in Humans." *Developmental Neuroscience*, Aug., 32:257-267, 2010.
38 Eisenberg, N., Fabes, R.A., & Spinrad, T.L. "Prosocial Development." In N. Eisenberg, W. Damon, & R. M. Lerner, eds., *Handbook of Child Psychology: Social, Emotional, and Personality Development*. Hoboken, NJ: John Wiley & Sons, Inc., 2006.
39 Decety, 2010.
40 *Ibid.*
41 *Ibid.*
42 Harris, P.L. "Children's understanding of emotion." In M. Lewis, J.M. Haviland-Jones, & L.F. Barrett, eds., *Handbook of Emotions*. New York: The Guilford Press, 2008.
43 Decety, 2010.
44 *Ibid.*
45 *Ibid.*
46 *Ibid.*
47 *Ibid.*
48 Panksepp, J. *Affective Neuroscience: The Foundations of Human and Animal Emotions*. Oxford: Oxford University Press, 1998.
49 Lego Toys, 1985.
50 *Ibid.*
51 Panksepp, 1998.
52 "Care for Kids." https://www.careforkids.com.au/blog/the-froebel-approach. Accessed May 26, 2023.
53 Singer, J. "Imaginative Play in Early Childhood: A Foundation for Adaptive Emotional and Cognitive Development." *International Medical Journal*, Vol. 5(2):93-100, 1998.
54 Shmukler, D. "Imaginative play in pre-school children as an indicator of emotional and cognitive development." *South African Journal of Psychology*, 9(1-2):37-41, 1979.
55 *Ibid.*
56 Gould, R., *Child Studies through Fantasy*. New York: Quadrangle Books, 1972.
57 Singer, 1998.
58 Drucker, J. "Toddler play: Some comments on its functions in the developmental process." *Psychoanalysis & Contemporary Science* 4,

479–527, 1975.
59. Crawley, S.B., & Sherrod, K.B. "Parent–infant play during the first year of life." *Infant Behavior & Development*, 7(1):65–75, 1984. DOI:. https://doi.org/10.1016/S0163-6383(84)80023-5.
60. Beaulieu, L., & Povinelli, J.L. "Improving solitary play with a typically developing preschooler." *Behavioral Interventions*, 33(2):212-218, 2018.
61. Katz, J.C., & Buchholz, E.S. ""I did it myself": The necessity of solo play for preschoolers." *Early Child Development and Care* 155:39–50, 1999. DOI: https://doi.org/10.1080/0030443991550104
62. Barnes, K.E. "Preschool play norms: A replication." *Developmental Psychology*, 5(1):99-103, 1971. DOI: https://doi.org/10.1037/h0031078
63. Lynch, H., Moore, A., Edwards, C., Horgan, L. "Advancing play participation for all: The challenge of addressing play diversity and inclusion in community parks and playgrounds." *British Journal of Occupational Therapy*, 83(2):107-117, 2020. DOI:10.1177/0308022619881936
64. McKinney, C., & Power, L. "Childhood playtime, parenting, and psychopathology in emerging adults: Implications for research and play therapists." *International Journal of Play Therapy*, 21(4):215-231, 2012. DOI: doi: http://dx.doi.org/10.1037/a0029172
65. Winerman, L. "Play in peril." *Monitor on Psychology*, September 2009.
66. Mallory, B.L., & New, R.S. "Social constructivist theory and principles of inclusion: Challenges for early childhood special education." *The Journal of Special Education*, 28(3):322–337, 1994. DOI: https://doi.org/10.1177/002246699402800307
67. Wieder, S. "The Power of Symbolic Play in Emotional Development through the DIR Lens." *Topics in Language Disorders*, 37(3):259-281, 2017.
68. Trehub, S.E. "The Maternal Voice as a Special Signal for Infants." In M. Filippa, P. Kuhn, & B. Westrup, eds., *Early Vocal Contact and Preterm Infant Brain Development*. Springer International Publishing AG, 2017. DOI: https://doi.org/10.1007/978-3-319-65077-7.
69. Page, M., Wilhelm, M.S., Gamble, W.C., & Card, N.A. "A comparison of maternal sensitivity and verbal stimulation as unique predictors of infant social–emotional and cognitive development." *Infant*

Behavior and Development, 33(1):101-110, 2010.
70 Dale, P.S., Tosto, M.G., Hayiou-Thomas, M.E., & Plomin, R. "Why does parental language input style predict child language development? A twin study of gene-environment correlation." *Journal of Communication Disorders,* 57:106-117, 2015. DOI: 10.1016/j.jcomdis.2015.07.004.
71 Hollenstein, T., Tighe, A.B., & Lougheed, J.P. "Emotional development in the context of mother–child relationships." *Current Opinion in Psychology,* Oct. 2017:140-144. DOI: 10.1016/j.copsyc.2017.07.010.
72 Cole, P.M. "Moving ahead in the study of the development of emotion regulation." *International Journal of Behavioral Development,* 38(2):203–207, 2014. DOI: https://doi.org/10.1177/0165025414522170.
73 Eisenberg, N., Cumberland, A., & Spinrad, T. L. "Parental Socialization of Emotion." *Psychological Inquiry,* 9:241-273, 1998. DOI: https://doi.org/10.1207/s15327965pli0904_1
74 Dworkin, J.B., Larson, R., & Hansen, D. "Adolescents' accounts of growth experiences in youth activities." *Journal of Youth and Adolescence,* 32(1):17-26, 2003.
75 Eccles, J., & Appleton Gootman, J. "Community Programs to Promote Youth Development." National Research Council, U.S., Institute of Medicine, 2002.
76 McLaughlin, M.W. "Community Counts: How Youth Organizations Matter for Youth Development." Publication Education Network, Washington, D.C. National Academy Press, 2000.
77 Anderson, J.C., Funk, J.B., Elliott, R., & Smith, P.H. "Parental support and pressure and children's extracurricular activities: Relationships with amount of involvement and affective experience of participation." *Journal of Applied Developmental Psychology,* 24(2):241-257, 2003.
78 Ehrlich, A. *The Random House Book of Fairy Tales* New York: Alfred Knopf, 1985.
79 Committee on Early Childhood, American Academy of Pediatrics, 1994.
80 Bowlby, J. *A Secure Base: Parent-Child Attachment and Healthy Human Development.* New York: Basic Books, 2008.
81 Center on the Developing Child, Harvard University. *What is Early*

Child Development? A Guide to the Science. Retrieved from https://developingchild.harvard.edu/guide/what-is-early-childhood-development-a-guide-to-the-science/, May 20, 2022.

82 Center on the Developing Child. "5 Steps For Brain Building Serve and Return." Harvard University, 2017. Retrieved from www.developingchild.harvard.edu, May 20, 2022.

83 Center on the Developing Child, Harvard University.

84 Meins, E., Fernyhough, C., Fradley, E., & Tuckey, M. "Rethinking Maternal Sensitivity: Mothers' Comments on Infants' Mental Processes Predict Security of Attachment at 12 Months." *Journal of Child Psychology & Psychiatry & Allied Disciplines*, 42(5):637, 2001. DOI: 10.1111/1469-7610.00759

85 Meins, E. "Sensitive attunement to infants' internal states: operationalizing the construct of mind-mindedness." *Attachment & Human Development*, 15(5/6):524–544, 2013. DOI: 10.1080/14616734.2013.830388

86 Ainsworth, M.D.S., Blehar, M.C., Waters, E., & Wall, S. *Patterns of Attachment: A Psychological Study of the Strange Situation*. Mahwah, NJ: Lawrence Erlbaum, 1978.

87 Ainsworth, M.D., Bell, S.M., & Stayton, D.J. "Individual differences in strange-situation behavior of one-year-olds." In H.R. Schaffer, ed. *The origins of human social relations.* Cambridge, Mass.: Academic Press, 1971; Ainsworth, M.D.S., Bell, S.M., & Stayton, D.F. "Infant-Mother Attachment and Social Development: "Socialization" as a Product of Reciprocal Responsiveness to Signals." In P.M. Richards, ed., *The Integration of a Child into a Social World*. Cambridge: Cambridge University Press, 1974.

88 Meins et al., 2001.

89 Ainsworth et al., 1971.

90 Ainsworth et al., 1974

91 Meins et al., 2001.

92 Goldberg, S., MacKay-Soroka, S., & Rochester, M. "Affect, attachment, and maternal responsiveness." *Infant Behavior and Development*, 17(3):335-339, 1994.

93 Goldberg, S., MacKay-Soroka, S., & Rochester, M. "Affect, attachment, and maternal responsiveness." Infant Behavior & Development,

17(3): 335–339, 1994. https://doi.org/10.1016/0163-6383(94)90013-2
94　Ainsworth et al., 1978.
95　*Ibid.*
96　Darling, N., & Steinberg, L. "Parenting style as context: An integrative model." *Psychological Bulletin*, 113(3):487–496, 1993. DOI: https://doi.org/10.1037/0033-2909.113.3.487
97　Akhtar, N., Dunham, F., & Dunham, P.J. "Directive interactions and early vocabulary development: The role of joint attentional focus." *Journal of Child Language*, 18(1):41–49, 1991. DOI: https://doi.org/10.1017/S0305000900013283; Tomasello, M., & Farrar, M.J. "Joint attention and early language." *Child Development*, 57(6):1454–1463, 1986. DOI: https://doi.org/10.2307/1130423
98　Smith, K.E., Landry, S.H., & Swank, P.R. "The influence of early patterns of positive parenting on children's preschool outcomes." *Early Education and Development*, 11(2):147–169, 2000. DOI: https://doi.org/10.1207/s15566935eed1102_2; Tamis-LeMonda, C.S., Bornstein M.H., & Baumwell, L. "Maternal Responsiveness and Children's Achievement of Language Milestones." *Child Development*, 72(3):748-767, 1989.
99　Landry, S.H., Smith, K.E., Swank, P.R., & Guttentag, C. "A responsive parenting intervention: the optimal timing across early childhood for impacting maternal behaviors and child outcomes." *Developmental Psychology*, 44(5):1335, 2008.
100　Dix, T. "The affective organization of parenting: Adaptive and maladaptive processes." *Psychological Bulletin*, 110(1):3-25, 1991. DOI: http://dx.doi.org.ezproxy1.lib.asu.edu/10.1037/0033-2909.110.1.3
101　Meins, E., Fernyhough, C., Russell, J., & Clark-Carter, D. "Security of attachment as a predictor of symbolic and mentalising abilities: a longitudinal study." *Social Development*, 7(1):1–24, 1998. DOI: 10.1111/1467-9507.00047
102　Dunn, J., Brown, J., Slomkowski, C., Tesla, C., & Youngblade, L. "Young Children's Understanding of Other People's Feelings and Beliefs: Individual Differences and Their Antecedents." *Child Development*, 62(6):1352-1366, 1991. DOI: https://doi.org/10.1111/j.1467-8624.1991.tb01610.x
103　Ainsworth et al., 1971; Fonagy, P., & Target, M. "The efficacy of

psychoanalysis for children with disruptive disorders." *Journal of the American Academy of Child & Adolescent Psychiatry*, 33(1):45–55, 1997. DOI: https://doi.org/10.1097/00004583-199401000-00007

104 Meins et al., 1998.

105 Stern, D.N. *The Interpersonal World of the Infant: A View From Psychoanalysis and Developmental Psychology*. New York: Basic Books, 1985.

106 Haft, W.L., & Slade, A. "Affect attunement and maternal attachment: A pilot study." *Infant Mental Health Journal*, 10(3):157-172, 1989.

107 Bowlby, 1969.

108 Duncan, L.G., Coatsworth, J.D., & Greenberg, M.T. "A Model of Mindful Parenting: Implications for Parent-Child Relationships and Prevention Research." *Clinical Child & Family Psychology Review*, 12(3):255–270, 2009. DOI: 10.1007/s10567-009-0046-3

109 Bögels, S., & Restifo, K. *Mindful Parenting: A Guide for Mental Health Practitioners*. New York: W.W. Norton & Company, 2014.

110 Moreira, H., Gouveia, M.J., & Canavarro, M.C. "Is mindful parenting associated with adolescents' well-being in early and middle/late adolescence? The mediating role of adolescents' attachment representations, self-compassion and mindfulness." *Journal of Youth and Adolescence*, 47(8):1771-1788, 2018. DOI: https://doi-org.ezproxy1.lib.asu.edu/10.1007/s10964-018-0808-7

111 Farrow, C., & Blissett, J. "Maternal mind-mindedness during infancy, general parenting sensitivity and observed child feeding behavior: a longitudinal study." *Attachment & Human Development*, 16(3):230–241, 2014. DOI: https://doi-org.ezproxy.lib.asu.edu/10.1080/14616734.2014.898158

112 Bums, B.M. and Maritz, Y. "Mindful parents, resilient children: The significance of compassion for parenting." In T.G. Plante, ed., *Maximize Compassion, Minimize Cruelty: Psychological, Spiritual, and Religious Influences*. New York: Praeger, 2015.

113 Winnicott, D.W. *The Child, the Family, and the Outside World*. London: Penguin, 1973.

114 Winnicott, D.W. *Winnicott on the child*. New York: Perseus Publishing, 2002.

115 Winnicott, D.W. *The Family and Individual Development*. London:

Routledge, 1965.
116 Nussbaum, M.C. *Philosophical Interventions: Reviews 1986-2011*. Oxford University Press, USA, 2012.
117 Casement, P. *Further Learning from the Patient*. London: Routledge, 1990.
118 Fonagy and Target, 1997.
119 Gilbert, P. "The origins and nature of compassion focused therapy." *British Journal of Clinical Psychology*, 53:6-41, 2014. Retrieved from https://self-compassion.org/wp-content/uploads/publications/GilbertCFT.pdf May 20, 2022.
120 Combs, A.W., *Perceptual Psychology: A Humanistic Approach to the Study of Persons*. New York: Harper & Row, 1976.
121 Rogers, C.R. *Carl Rogers on personal power*. New York: Delacorte, 1977.
122 Corey, G. *Theory and Practice of Counseling and Psychotherapy*. Monterey, CA: Brooks Cole Publishing Company, 1986
123 *Ibid.*
124 *Ibid.*
125 Rogers, 1977.
126 Rogers, C.R. *On Becoming a Person. A Therapist's View of Psychotherapy*. New York: Houghton Mifflin Company, 1961.
127 Standal, S. *The need for positive regard: A contribution to client-centered theory*. Unpublished PhD. thesis, University of Chicago. 1954.
128 Buber, M. Ich und Du [I and Thou], Leipzig: Insel Verlag, 1923.
129 Friedman, M. *To Deny our Nothingness: Contemporary Images of Man*. London: Victor Gollancz, 1967.
130 Internet Encyclopedia of Philosophy.
131 Friedman, M. *Martin Buber's Life and Work*, Detroit, MI: Wayne State University Press, 1988
132 Friedman, M. "Buber and dialogical therapy: Healing through meeting." *The Humanistic Psychologist*, 36(3-4): 298-315, 2008. DOI: https://doi.org/10.1080/08873260802350014
133 Plant, K.L. "The Two Worlds of Martin Buber." *Theology*, 88(724): 281–287, 1985. DOI: https://doi.org/10.1177/0040571X8508800406
134 Friedman, 2008.
135 *Ibid.*
136 Friedman, M. *Encounter on the narrow ridge: A life of Martin Buber*. St.

Paul, MN: Paragon House Publishers, 1991.
137 Kramer, K.P. *Marin Buber's Dialogue, Discovering Who We Really Are.* Eugene, OR: Cascade Books, 2019.
138 Zemelka, A.M. "Alcmaeon of Croton - Father of Neuroscience? Brain, Mind and Senses in the Alcmaeon's Study" (sic). *Journal of Neurology and Neuroscience*, 8(3), 2017.
139 American Psychological Association, 2015.
140 Ackerman, S. *Discovering the Brain.* Washington, DC: National Academies Press (US), 1992.
141 *Ibid.*
142 Center on the Development of the Child, 2012.
143 Trevarthen, C. "What it is like to be a person who knows nothing? Defining the active intersubjective mind of a newborn human being." *Infant and Child Development*, 20(1):119-135, 2011. DOI: https://doi.org/10.1002/icd.689
144 Stone, L., Underwood, C., & Hotchkiss, J. "The Relational Habitus: Intersubjective Processes in Learning Settings." *Human Development*, 55(2): 65–91, 2012. DOI:10.1159/000337150
145 Bråten, S., & Trevarthen, C. "Prologue: From infant intersubjectivity and participant movements to simulation and conversation in cultural common sense." In S. Bråten, ed., *On Being Moved: From Mirror Neurons to Empathy.* Amsterdam: John Benjamins Publishing Company, 2007. DOI: https://doi.org/10.1075/aicr.68.04bra
146 Wiktionary.
147 Trevarthen, C. "Learning About Ourselves From Children: Why A Growing Human Brain Needs Interesting Companions." *Research and Clinical Centre for Child Development, Annual Report 2002-2003* No. 26:9-44. Graduate School of Education, Hokkaido University, 2003.
148 Trevarthen, C. "The self born in intersubjectivity: The psychology of an infant communicating." In U. Neisser, ed., *The Perceived Self: Ecological and Interpersonal Sources of Self-Knowledge.* Cambridge: Cambridge University Press, 1993.
149 *Ibid.*
150 Ammaniti, M. & Gallese, V. *The Birth Of Intersubjectivity: Psychodynamics, Neurobiology, and the Self.* New York: W.W. Norton & Company, 2014.

151 *Ibid.*
152 Lorenz, K. "Die angeborenen Formen möglicher Erfahrung." *Zeitschrift für Tierpsychologie*, 5(2):235-409, 1943.
153 Bowlby, 1969.
154 Ammaniti & Gallese, 2014.
155 *Ibid.*
156 Gallese, V. "The roots of empathy: the shared manifold hypothesis and the neural basis of intersubjectivity." *Psychopathology*. 36(4):171-80, 2003. DOI: 10.1159/000072786. PMID: 14504450; Gallese, V., Keysers, C., & Rizzolatti, G. "A unifying view of the basis of social cognition." *Trends in Cognitive Science*, 8(9):396-403, 2004. DOI: 10.1016/j.tics.2004.07.002.
157 Ammaniti & Gallese, 2014.
158 Tanaka, S. "Intercorporeality as a theory of social cognition". *Theory and Psychology* 2015, 25(4): 455-472. DOI: 10.1177/0959354315583035
159 Ammaniti & Gallese, 2014.
160 *Ibid.*
161 Gallese, V. "The inner sense of action: Agency and motor representations." *Journal of Consciousness Studies*, 7(10):23–40, 2000; Gallese, V., Rochat, M., Cossu, G., & Sinigaglia, C. "Motor cognition and its role in the phylogeny and ontogeny of action understanding." *Developmental Psychology*, 45(1):103–113, 2009. DOI: https://doi.org/10.1037/a0014436
162 Ammaniti & Gallese, 2014.
163 Wilson, D. "Metarepresentation in Linguistic Communication." In D. Sperber, ed., *Metarepresentations: A Multidisciplinary Perspective*. Oxford: Oxford University Press, 2000.
164 Ammaniti & Gallese, 2014.
165 *Ibid.*
166 Tossani, E. "The Concept of Mental Pain." *Laboratory of Psychosomatics and Clinimetrics*, 82(2):67-73, 2013. DOI: 10.1159/000343003. Epub 2012 Dec 22. PMID 23295405.
167 Bakan, D. *Disease, pain, and sacrifice: Toward a psychology of suffering*. Chicago: University of Chicago Press, 1968.
168 Kross, E., Berman, M.G., Mischel, W., Smith, E.E, & Wager, T.D. "Social rejection shares somatosensory representations with

physical pain." *PNAS*, 108(15), 2011. DOI: https://doi.org/10.1073/pnas.1102693108

169   Eisenberger, N.I., & Lieberman, M.D. "Why It Hurts to Be Left Out: The Neurocognitive Overlap Between Physical and Social Pain." In K.D. Williams, J.P. Forgas, & W. von Hippel, eds., *The Social Outcast: Ostracism, Social Exclusion, Rejection, and Bullying*. London: Psychology Press, 2005.

170   Zhang, M., Zhang, Y., & Kong, Y. "Interaction between social pain and physical pain." *Brain Science Advances*, 5(4): 2165-273, 2019. DOI: https://doi.org/10.26599/BSA.2019.9050023.

171   Panksepp, J. & Biven, L. (with Siegel, D.J.) *The archaeology of mind: neuroevolutionary origins of human emotions*. New York: W.W. Norton, 2012.

172   Kross et al., 2011.

173   Zhang et al., 2019.

174   Nelson III, C.A., Fox, N.A., Zeanah, Jr., C.H. "Anguish of the Abandoned Child." *Scientific American*, 308(4):6207, 2013. DOI: 10.1038/scientificamerican0413-62. PMID: 23539791.

175   Nelson et al., 2013.

176   *Ibid.*

177   *Ibid.*

178   Eisenberger, N.I., Lieberman, M.D., & Williams, K.D. "Does Rejection Hurt? An fMRI Study of Social Exclusion." *Science* 2003 Oct 10, 302(5643):290-2, 2003. DOI: 10.1126/science. 1089134. PMID: 14551436.

ABOUT THE AUTHOR

RONALD RUFF, PhD, began working with children and parents in 1969. He started his private practice in 1974 and continued until 2017. During that time, he worked with a diverse range of age groups; cultural, educational, socioeconomic, and racial backgrounds; and diagnostic classifications, garnering extensive experience in psychological treatment, assessment, and consultation in health care, education, government, judicial systems, training, teaching, and research.

Dr. Ruff was awarded a fellowship to the Harvard Medical School Department of Psychiatry and Cambridge Hospital, Center for Addictive Studies. He served as Clinical Director of a residential treatment center for children, as Chief Psychologist of a community mental health center, on the staff of several psychiatric hospitals, as a juvenile court psychologist, as Director of Clinical Internship Training, and as an adjunct instructor who taught psychology doctoral students. He received a BA in Psychology with French studies from Oberlin College, an MS in Counseling Psychology from George Williams College, and a PhD in Clinical Psychology from Illinois Institute of Technology. He has been married for fifty-three years and has three daughters and four grandchildren.

Printed in the USA
CPSIA information can be obtained
at www.ICGtesting.com
LVHW052028230524
781104LV00006B/33

9 781960 378187